PN1995.2 FER

CINEMA

and History

Contemporary Film Studies

General Editor
Patricia Erens
Rosary College

CINEMA

and *History*

MARC FERRO

**Translated by
Naomi Greene**

Wayne State University Press • Detroit   1988

The translator wishes to thank Carol Gibbons of the
University of California, Santa Barbara, library for her help
with the research.

Library of Congress Cataloging-in-Publication Data

Ferro, Marc.
  [Cinéma et histoire. English]
  Cinema and history / Marc Ferro; translated by Naomi
Greene.
     p.   cm.—(Contemporary film studies)
  Translation of: Cinéma et histoire.
  Bibliography: p.
  Includes index.
  ISBN 0-8143-1904-1 (alk. paper). ISBN 0-8143-1905-X
(pbk. : alk. paper)
  1. Motion pictures and history. I. Title. II. Series.
PN1995.2.F413 1988
791.43'09'09358—dc19   87-37213
                                                    CIP

CONTENTS

Contents

Chapter 6
Analysis of Societies and Different Types of Films
81

FILM: AGENT OF HISTORY

Chapter 7
Concentration Camps in the Soviet Union:
An Information Breach
107

Chapter 8
On American Anti-Nazism, 1939–43: Fragments
111

Chapter 9
Does an Anti-militarist Cinema Exist?
118

SOCIETY WHICH PRODUCES, SOCIETY WHICH RECEIVES

Chapter 10
Conflict Within *The Third Man*
125

Chapter 11
La grande illusion and Its Receptions
132

MODES OF ACTION OF CINEMATOGRAPHIC LANGUAGE

Chapter 12
Dissolves in *Jud Süss*
139

Contents

TRANSLATOR'S PREFACE

This book is a translation of almost all the essays in French historian Marc Ferro's *Cinéma et histoire* (Paris: Denoel, 1977), many of which have been revised in recent years. Chapter 6 appeared in Ferro's *Analyse de film, analyse de sociétés: Une source nouvelle pour l'Histoire* (Paris: Hachette, 1975). Chapter 16 is a new version of a shorter essay written for the Spanish translation of *Cinéma et histoire, Cine e Historia* (Barcelona: Gili, 1980). Chapter 5 was published in *Nordic Journal of Soviet and East European Studies*, Vol. 3, No. 2 (1986); Chapter 14 in *Film et Histoire*, ed. Marc Ferro (Paris: Ecole des Hautes Etudes en Sciences Sociales, 1984). Marc Ferro has determined the order of the essays and written the following chapters for the present volume: part two of Chapter 4 (on Abel Gance's *Napoléon*), Chapter 15, and the concluding "Proposition for a Global Classification of Films in their Relationship to History." Translator's notes have been added to clarify allusions which might have seemed obscure to American readers.

In all of these essays—which range over the length and breadth of film history—Ferro returns to central questions: What

11

can cinema tell us about the spirit, or "mentalité," of an era? In what ways does cinema constitute a valuable document for the study of history, a document long overlooked by "official" historians? Finally, in what zones and modes do cinema and history intersect? In his exploration of these intersections, Ferro places concrete and often detailed analyses within broader theoretical perspectives. Although, of course, the overlappings are intricate and many, each major division of the book focuses on one aspect of these intersections.

At the heart of all these intersections lies film's status as, in Ferro's words, both an "agent" and a "source" of history. As a "source" of history, it is often ignored by "real" historians. Yet, as Ferro shows in his analyses of early Soviet films and of Abel Gance's *Napoléon*, film not only reveals a great deal about the external aspects of a historical moment (for example, what places and people looked like), but also may indicate more than "official" historical documents about ideological trends or social attitudes and beliefs. Such indications may not even be conscious. This is the case, demonstrates Ferro, in such important Soviet films as *Chapayev* and *Dura Lex*. On the surface both films appeared to exhibit the avowed values of Soviet Russia, but beneath both of these films Ferro discerns ideologies that endorse different values and raise disquieting issues about the Soviet state. Film may even come to replace "history" itself, as *Battleship Potemkin* has, when the imaginative re-creation of history is more "real" than the "historical fact." So strong is the imprint of *Potemkin* upon our minds that when we think of the Russian Revolution, we think of scenes that may have never occurred.

But a film that is now a "source" of history may also have been an "agent" that helped shape history's course. In Chapter 8 Ferro shows that this was the case for several films made shortly before and after 1940; these films were historical "agents" which prompted us to "choose" our friends and enemies at the time of World War II. Now, however, these very films are a "source" of history since they reveal our attitudes to us. Sometimes these attitudes are disquieting: Chapter 14 reveals the depth and persistence of certain racist currents in the United States.

In Part III Ferro looks at the receptions accorded films and production conditions in relation to history and ideology. The same film may receive different receptions at different moments in history, indicating changes in the society which looks at it. In this context, Ferro examines one of Renoir's greatest films, *La grande illusion*, which received a very different reception before World War II than it did afterwards. Or, as in the case of *The Third Man*, a film may be marked by the conflicting (and often unacknowledged) ideologies of its various collaborators.

The last part of *Cinema and History* examines the way specific cinematic devices or procedures interact with history. Ferro's analyses of the "dissolves" in *Jud Süss* indict its director for anti-Semitism; the choice of interviewees in Marcel Ophül's *Le chagrin et la pitié* creates an "opaque" ideology; Fritz Lang's transposition of a real incident in *M* tells a great deal about the Weimar Republic and the rise of Nazism.

Cinema and History comes at a welcome time: as history is once more assuming a central role in film criticism, Ferro's book makes us question the vision of the past given us by "official" history at the same time that it opens new perspectives for the study of film.

Naomi Greene

INTRODUCTION

Film as Source and Agent of History

The intersecting points between cinema and history are numerous. They occur at the junction where History is being made and where it is perceived as an account of our era or as an explanation of the development of societies. Cinema intervenes in all of these places. First of all film acts as a *historical agent*. Chronologically, it first appeared as an instrument for scientific progress. The accomplishments of Eadweard Muybridge and of Etienne-Jules Marey were presented to the Academy of Sciences.[1] This original function has been retained by today's cinema and has been extended to medicine. It was also used by military institutions to identify an enemy's weapons.

In a similar way, when the cinema became an art its pioneers intervened in history in their fictional or documentary films, which used the pretext of telling a story in order to indoctrinate and glorify. In England, they essentially showed the Queen with her empire and navy. In France they chose to film what the rising bourgeoisie produced—a train, an exhibition, republican institutions. Propaganda also appeared in fictional films from the

Mile End Library
Queen Mary, University of London

Borrowed Items 08/02/2011 19:42
XXXXX8076

Item Title	Due Date
History in exile : memory and	09/02/2011
The Balkans : from the end :	09/02/2011
Imagining the Balkans	09/02/2011
* Cinema and history	15/02/2011
* Writing history in film	08/03/2011
* The historical film : history	15/02/2011

Amount Outstanding : £1.50

* Indicates items borrowed today

PLEASE NOTE
If you still have overdue books on loan
you may have more fines to pay

beginning—films were for or against Dreyfus, denounced the Boxers, etc.

As soon as the rulers of a society understood the role that cinema could play, they tried to use it for their own purposes. Since this same attitude was shared by both Western and Eastern rulers, the differences that do exist here are found at the level of awareness, not at that of ideology. But this can be confusing. Authorities—whether they represent capital, the Soviets, or bureaucracy—would like to subjugate cinema. Filmmakers, however, believe it can be autonomous and can act as a counterforce, a little like the way the press operates in the United States and Canada, or the way writers have always acted. Consciously or not, these filmmakers are doubtlessly like anyone else who serves a cause or an ideology either explicitly or without asking themselves questions. But this does not exclude the fact that some of them do resist, and struggle bitterly in defense of their own ideas. In their own ways, the Jean Vigo of *Zéro de conduite* [*Zero for Conduct*, 1933], the René Clair of *A nous la liberté* [1931], the Louis Malle of *Lacombe Lucien* [1973], and the Alain Resnais of *Stavisky* [1974]—to say nothing of almost all the films Godard has made—reveal an independence vis-à-vis dominant ideological currents. They create and offer a vision of an unseen world, a world of their own which arouses a new awareness with such force that existing ideological institutions (political parties, churches, etc.) struggle with and back away from these works as if these institutions and they alone had the right to express themselves in the name of God, the nation, or the proletariat—as if only they enjoyed a legitimacy apart from the one they took for themselves.

This ability of cinema continues to surprise even those churches most ensconced in their dogmatic certitudes, which are, moreover, often based upon subverted cultures. This explains the extraordinary adventures of a certain number of Soviet filmmakers who can produce films whose meaning and construction cannot be grasped by the visually illiterate bureaucratic apparatchiks who still judge a work's ideology in terms of its dialogue or its scenario—its written trace.

Yesterday, the proliferation of super 8 cameras and today

the half-inch video have created a new era. The cinema can become an even more active agent of social or cultural awareness since society is no longer merely an object to be analyzed like someone who plays at being the good savage for the benefit of a new colonizer: the militant cameraman. Formerly the "object" to be analyzed by an "avant-garde," society can henceforth assume responsibility for itself. This could be the meaning of the transition from films by militants to militant film.

Although measuring or evaluating the influence of cinema is difficult, at least certain sequences of cause and effect can be observed. We know that *Jud Süss* [*Jew Seuss*, Veidt Harlan, 1940] was a great success in Germany above and beyond Goebbel's order that it be widely shown. We also know that just after it was shown in Marseilles, Jews were molested. We can note, too, that the success of anti-Nazi films and films exalting patriotic solidarity in the United States were successful only if they did not glorify either the Resistance in occupied countries, or the struggle against legal institutions in Germany; and if, on the pretext of better coordinating production following Roosevelt's appeal, they didn't question the free initiative of every undertaking.

Correlations and evidence of this sort are rare. However, a recent episode bears witness to the effectiveness of the cinematographic fact. The O.R.T.F.'s [French television] presentation of a Latvian film on labor camps in the Soviet Union provoked the French Communist party to take a stand critical of the camps—something it had managed to avoid doing until then.

Cinema intervenes by means of a certain number of modes of action that render the film effective and operative. As we will see, this ability is undoubtedly linked to the society that produces films and that receives and takes delivery of them. It is true that, above and beyond the way non-cinematographic constraints (conditions of production, forms of commercialization, choice of genre) function in cinema, film disposes of a certain number of modes of expression. These do not merely transcribe literary writing, but have their own specificity that has been studied by theoreticians of cinematic writing from Jean Mitry to Bruce Morissette and Christian Metz.

However, it would be an illusion to imagine that the practice of this cinematographic language is innocent, even unconsciously. Of course, it is easy to see that a theoretician of cinema, such as Godard, retains more control over his writing and his "style" than someone else. The long traveling shot of *Weekend* [Jean-Luc Godard, 1967] restores real time in the midst of different temporalities that are placed in the film to create an "effect" and render unbearable the situation imagined by the filmmaker. In the same way, a device seemingly used to express duration—or some other stylistic figure transcribing a shift in space—may reveal, unbeknownst to the filmmaker, ideological and social zones of which he was not necessarily aware, or that he believed he had repressed. This is the case in the dissolves of *Jud Süss* (which are analyzed in Chapter 12). In the same way we can study the effects of montage (as Kuleshov and Eisenstein and others have already done), the way different elements in the sound track function, and so forth. Chris Marker showed how this could be done in *Lettre de Sibérie* [*Letter from Siberia*, 1958]. Today, others systematically analyze the various possible combinations within a film.

Thus, the utilization and practice of specific modes of writing are weapons that are linked to the society which produces the film and which receives it. The latter makes itself felt first of all by censorship—all forms of censorship, including censorship per se and self-censorship. The epilogue of F. W. Murnau's *Der letzte Mann* [*The Last Laugh*, 1924], for example, was added because the producer did not want the unfortunate doorman of the Atlantic Hotel to end his life in degradation and solitude. Such an end would have discredited the society and the regime—in this case, the Weimar Republic—that allowed it to occur. Other happy endings are not due, as in this case, to a ukase of the producer. But they too have been added just the same, since morality—a certain kind of morality—must triumph. Another kind of film, designed as a documentary, which seemingly seeks to be objective by striking a balance between opposing views, is informed by the same sort of concession to a kind of censorship which, in this case, is inverted: Ophüls, Harris, and Sédouy in *Le chagrin et la pitié* [*The Sorrow and the Pity*, 1971] always let Mendès-France or a Communist speak as a concession to the producer or to the public's supposed and created needs. But they always give the last word to someone on the Right who is thereby enabled to make the most of it.

It is easy to imagine that making a film creates secret rivalries, conflicts, and struggles for control. We have known this since *Ivan the Terrible* [Sergei Eisenstein, 1941 pt. I, 1946 pt. II]. This was true then and it has remained true. Covertly or explicitly these conflicts create disputes—according to the society involved—involving the artist and the state, the producer and the distributors, the author and the filmmakers, as well as the different members of the crew or different crews, according to systems that vary for each production and for each work. These are rarely discernible, except in the form of vague allusions concerning the "ambiance" of shooting or realization. We will study in Chapter 10 the visible or repressed conflicts that emerge from a reading of *The Third Man* [Sir Carol Reed, 1949].

Thus like every cultural product, political action, and business, each film has a history that is History, with its network of personal relationships, its order of objects and men where privileges and burdens, hierarchies and honors are regulated. The benefits of glory and money, the wars or guerrilla fighting which take place among actors, directors, technicians, and producers (warfare which is all the more cruel since it takes place under the flags of art and liberty and within the closeness of a shared adventure) are regulated here with precision, like the rites of a feudal charter. No business, military, political, or religious undertaking experiences such an intolerable gap between the splendor and good fortune of some of the people involved and the gloomy misery of others.

Years ago Eisenstein observed that every society receives its images in function of its own culture. While the allegory of the slaughter in *Strike* [*Stachka*, Eisenstein, 1925] created the desired effect in cities, in the countryside the peasants, accustomed to such bloodshed, remained indifferent. Let us add to Eisenstein's remark that the peasants also lacked the education that would have allowed them to grasp an allegory—obviously.

Moreover, a phenomenon of this sort must be analyzed not only in terms of different civilizations (city/country, East/West, whites/blacks) seen diachronically, but also within the heart of one culture. All this is called into play when we see how a figure of writing or style may be in or out of fashion, may remain in favor with one public or another which itself changes. The same is true of a work's content and meaning, which may be read in varying and contrary ways at two different points in its history. The first example is that of Abel Gance's *Napoléon* [1927] and, more recently, *La grande illusion* [*Grand Illusion*, Jean Renoir, 1937] (which is analyzed in Chapter 11 from this perspective). The latter film, which attempted to be pacifist, left-wing, and internationalist and was greeted as such in 1938, was reconsidered in 1946 (and afterward) and seen as a profoundly ambiguous work which was, in some sense, prematurely pro-Vichy and completely cut off from the permanent values of the Left.

A change in any single element of a film may change its meaning. In *Lénine par Lénine* [*Lenin on Lenin*, 1970], Pierre Samson accompanied the final sequence with a choral orchestration by Ernst Busch that prophetically announced the coming triumph of world revolution. On television, without consulting the filmmakers, O.R.T.F. censored the film by replacing the music with a Russian revolutionary song that was ostensibly more appropriate. At the beginning of the 1920s, this song certainly had lost none of its force. As an accompaniment to revolutionary images in 1970 it functioned differently, since it merely told the audience that the film was over.

A film's dynamic and social power, the forms its influence assumes, and its variable readings are all problems that may be linked. This was shown by a presentation in 1976 of *Der Fuchs von Glenarvon* [*The Fox of Glenarvon*, Max Kimmich], a film made late in 1940 that decries the genocide of the Irish by the English. This makes the anti-Nazi viewer of 1976 feel uneasy. He wants to be critical of the film's explicit ideology, but not at the cost of becoming an executioner of the Irish. Caught in this trap, he can see how this film functioned as an exorcism in 1940. The Germans could not believe themselves guilty of crimes that were exactly those they denounced, condemned, and combated.

The historical reading of a film and the cinematographic reading of history: these are the last two axes to be followed by anyone investigating the relationship between cinema and history. A cinematographic reading of history presents the historian with the problem of his own reading of the past. The experiences of several contemporary filmmakers (such as René Allio) making fictional as well as nonfictional films show that, thanks to popular memory and oral traditions, the historian-filmmaker can give back to society a history it has been deprived of by the institution of History. This point has been rightly emphasized by Michel Foucault in *Cahiers du cinéma*. But if you go further back than a century or two, the distance becomes excessive and the problem is quite different. *Battleship Potemkin* [*Bronenosts Potyomkin*, Eisenstein, 1925] and *Alexander Nevsky* [Eisenstein, 1938] are films in which the historical element is entirely different.

The historical and social reading of film undertaken in 1967 has permitted us to reach nonvisible zones in the past of societies—to reveal self-censorship or *lapses* (which remain in the unconscious of participants and witnesses) at work within a society or an artistic creation (see the analysis in Chapter 1 of *Dura Lex* [*Po zakonu* (*By the Law*), Lev Kuleshov, 1926]), or even the social content of bureaucratic practices during the Stalin era (see the study of *Chapayev* [Sergei and Georgy Vasiliev, 1934] in Chapter 3).

(1976)

NOTES

1. [Translator's Note: Eadweard Muybridge was a nineteenth century English photographer who, in 1881, invented a forerunner of moving pictures, the zoopraxiscope, which projected animated pictures on a screen. Etienne-Jules Marey was the French inventor of the chronophotographe, which directly inspired Lumière's Cinématographe, a camera and projector in one, first demonstrated in 1895.]

FILM: SOURCE OF HISTORY

CHAPTER 1

Film: A Counteranalysis of Society?

Historians and Cinema

Could film be an undesirable document for the historian? Almost a century old but ignored, it does not even rank among leftover sources. It does not enter the historian's mental universe. Actually, cinema was not yet born when history assumed its habits, perfected its method, and ceased to narrate in favor of explaining. The "language" of cinema appears unintelligible. Like that of dreams, its interpretation is uncertain. But this explanation will not satisfy someone who knows the indefatigable fervor of historians bent on discovering new domains, their ability to make tree trunks and old skeletons talk, and their readiness to consider essential what they previously deemed uninteresting.

As far as film—one more unwritten source—is concerned, we believe that its neglect does not involve an inability or a delay, but a blindness and an unconscious refusal that come from more complex causes. By examining which "monuments of the past" the historian has transformed into documents, and then "which documents the contemporary historian transforms into monuments,"[1] we can begin to understand and see why film plays no role.

Has it been said often enough that by asking himself about his work, by questioning *how* he writes History, the historian has wound up by forgetting to analyze his own function? Reading historians of History, one realizes that if the ideology of historians has varied and if several races of historians cohabit and constitute milieus that scarcely recognize each other but which nonetheless are identified by non-historians due to specific signs in their discourses, then their function has scarcely changed. Few historians—from Otto of Freising to Voltaire, from Polybius to Ernest Lavisse, from Tacitus to Mommsen—exist who, in the name of knowledge or science, have not served the prince, the state, a class, the nation—in short, an order (or system) that may or may not still exist. There have been few historians who, consciously or not, have not been its priests or its soldiers.[2]

Training the prince and the ruling milieus to govern well; teaching the people to obey; seeking, with or without them, History's direction and laws in order to understand them better— all these instances reveal a concern for effectiveness. Historians have always worked on behalf of the state that hired them. Leonardo Bruni in Florence and Etienne Pasquier in Paris counseled historians to abandon the Latin language in favor of the vulgate since "this would make them more effective." At the beginning of the twentieth century when, always on behalf of the state, historians glorified the nation, ministerial directives let them know that if the teaching of history did not achieve results, "the teacher could consider his time wasted."[3]

Histories of History confirm another fact. The historian— according to the nature of his mission and his era—chooses a given ensemble of sources and adopts a given method. He changes them just as a soldier changes weapons and tactics when those formerly considered useful lose their effectiveness. This observation has been recently confirmed by the adventure of post World War II Polish historiography which—because sources were lacking, lost, had disappeared, or had been deliberately destroyed by German and Soviet occupation—discovered in the products of material civilization unpublished documentary material allowing it to demonstrate the identity of the Polish nation

24

and its right to the western and eastern borders to which it laid claim.

Certainly we knew that no one wrote history innocently, but this opinion seems to have been confirmed in the early 1900s when cinematography began to appear. On the eve of World War I, historians—like their comrades the lawyers, bureaucrats, philosophers, and doctors—were already outfitted and ready for the fight. At that time the same historians wrote for both adults and children. It is interesting to recall the directives made by a French historian, Ernest Lavisse:

> It is incumbent upon history teachers to have the glorious duty of making the country . . . as well as all our past heroes, even those cloaked in legend, loved and understood. . . . If the schoolchild doesn't take away with him the living memory of our national glories, if he doesn't know that our ancestors fought upon a thousand battlefields for noble causes, if he hasn't at all learned the cost in blood and effort of achieving national unity . . . and creating from the chaos of our ancient institutions the sacred laws which render us free, if he doesn't become a citizen imbued with his duties and a soldier who loves his flag, the teacher will have wasted his time.[4]

"Glorious duty," "heroes . . . cloaked in legend," "noble causes," "national unity," "sacred laws which render us free," "soldier"— with slight differences these terms and the principles they represent were also found all over Europe in Kovalevski, Treitschke, and Seeley. France was not the only one to "enter the tricolor era." At that time the recognized historian used sources that constituted a corpus as carefully hierarchical as the society for which his work was intended. Like this society, documents were divided into categories in which the privileged classes, déclassés, plebians, and the Lumpenproletariat were easily distinguishable. As Benedetto Croce wrote, "history is always contemporary." At the beginning of the twentieth century this hierarchy reflected power relationships. Leading the procession were prestigious state archives—holding manuscripts or printed matter and unique documents—which expressed the state's power, as well as that of houses, parliaments, and financial chambers. This was followed by the no-longer-secret band of printed matter: legal and legislative texts that originally expressed power, then newspapers and publications emanating not only from it [i.e., Power] but also from the whole of cultivated society. Biographies, sources of local history, and travelers' tales formed the procession's tail. Even if such testimonies were worthy of belief, they occupied a humbler position in the elaboration of the thesis. History was perceived from the viewpoint of those who assumed responsibility for society: statesmen, diplomats, magistrates, businessmen, and administrators. They were the same ones who contributed to "national unity" and "to the writing of the sacred laws which render us free." At a time when centralization was reinforcing the power of the state and of the rulers of capital; when capitalism's hold was growing; when the people on one side of the Rhine were being persuaded that Berlin was as great as Rome while those on the other side of the river were being persuaded that Paris was the new Athens; when the European conflict was ticking away; when a pacifist or bellicose frenzy was infiltrating ideology; when philosophers, jurists, and historians were already being mobilized: in what way could folklore—whose survival attests precisely that the cultural unification of the country was not totally achieved—be useful to history? In what way could a little bit of film showing *a train coming into the station of La Ciotat be useful to History?*[5]

At the beginning of the twentieth century how did intelligent and educated people view cinematography? "A machine for stupidity and dissolution, a pastime for illiterates and miserable creatures worn down by their toil." Bishops, generals, notaries, professors, and magistrates shared this opinion of Georges Duhamel. They would not commit themselves to "this spectacle for slaves." Early legal opinions are a good indication of the reception accorded film by the ruling classes. Film was considered a sort of street attraction. The law did not even recognize authorship. Moving images were due to "a special machine by means of which they are obtained." For a long time the law considered that the author of a film was the person who wrote the scenario.[6] From force of habit the authorship rights of the person who filmed it were not recognized. He did not have the status of a cultivated man. He was deemed an image "hound," a hunter of images. Even today the man behind the camera remains anonymous where newsreels are concerned. Images are signed with the name of the firm that produces them—Pathé, Fox.[7] Thus in the eyes of jurists, learned people, leaders of society, and the state what is not written—the image—has no identity. How could historians refer to the image or even quote it? Without principles, an orphan prostituting itself to the populace, the image could not take its place among the great personages—legal points, commercial agreements, ministerial declarations, operational directives, speeches—which constitute society in the eyes of historians. Moreover, how could newsreels be trusted when everyone knows that these images, these false representations of reality, are deliberately selected and easily transformed; or that they are assembled by an unverifiable montage, a trick, an effect. Historians cannot base their work upon documents of this sort. Everyone knows that they work in glass cages and use "references and proofs." No one would think that the choice of their documents, the way they are assembled, and the way their issues are presented are just as much a montage, a trick, an effect. Has the possibility of consulting the same sources meant that all historians have written the same history of the French Revolution?

Fifty years have gone by. History has changed and film is still at the threshold of the laboratory. Certainly in 1970 the "elite" and "cultivated" people go to the movies. So does the historian, but (unconsciously?) he goes there like everyone else— merely as a spectator. In the meantime the Marxist revolution has taken place, transforming conceptions of History. With it, another method, another system, and another hierarchy of sources have prevailed. The Marxist historian looks behind political power seeking the base of the historical process in the analysis of modes of production and the class struggle. At the same time we have seen the birth of the social sciences, proud of their methods. However, like non-Marxists, Marxists retained several habits of the historian's ancient trade: they used a privileged way of placing things into perspective and a principle of selectivity concerning historical sources. Before long, and before it reintegrated the contribution of multiple human sciences, History exploded, the profession changed, and the very notion of the time of History was modified. In 1968 Francois Furet wrote: "Today's historian has ceased being a one-man band who can say everything about everything from the heights of the indeterminacy and the universality of his knowledge: history. He has ceased to tell what has happened; that is, he has ceased to select—among what has happened—whatever seems appropriate to his narrative, his taste, or his interpretation. Like his colleagues in other human sciences, he must say what he is seeking, compose the materials pertinent to his argument, present his hypotheses, his results, his proofs, his uncertainties."[8] Analyzing structures rather than events, he became interested in invisible, permanent structures and in transformations, realizing that, over a long time span, structures partially eclipse events. From that time on, materials allowing us to compose long curves—of prices, of demographic series—constituted the historian's favorite prey. He got his perforated cards, his code. In this world where the calculator is queen, where the computer reigns, what can a little image do? Where can Charlot [Chaplin] manage to get lost?

Furthermore, what is a film if not an event, an anecdote, a fiction, some censored information, or a newsreel that lumps together this winter's fashions and this summer's deaths? What can the new history do with this? The Right is fearful, the Left suspicious: has not the dominant ideology turned cinema into a "dream factory"? Has not a filmmaker, Jean-Luc Godard, asked himself if "cinema wasn't invented to camouflage reality from the masses"?[9] What false image of reality is offered—either by this gigantic industry in the West, or by the all-controlling state in the East? Of what reality is cinema really the image?

These doubts and questions are legitimate but they serve historians as alibis. For in the end censorship is always present and vigilant, transferred from writing to film and, within film, from the text to the image. It is not enough to observe that cinema fascinates and disturbs. Public forces and private powers intuit that it can have a corrosive effect. They realize that, even when closely watched, a film may be a witness. Newsreel or fiction, the image of reality offered by cinema appears terribly true. We realize that it does not necessarily correspond to the assertions of rulers, to the schemas of theorists, to the analysis of the opposition. Instead of supporting their remarks, it may reveal them as absurd. It is understandable that churches supervise, that priests of every religion and teachers of every profession manifest a supercilious and fanatical exigency regarding these moving images that they have not learned to analyze, control, and exploit in their speeches. The effect of film is to de-structure what several generations of men of state and thinkers have built into such a beautiful harmony. It destroys the alter image that every institution and every individual composes for itself in the face of society. The camera reveals their real functioning and tells more about each one of these than they could want. It unveils secrets and shows the underside of a society and its lapses.[10] It attacks society's structures. Nothing more is needed for a time of scorn to give way to a time of suspicion and fear. For the educated people of the twentieth century, this product of nature—the image, sound images—was not part of a language or a language system [*langue ou langage*]; it did not have its own culture and intelligibility. The idea that a gesture could be a sentence, a look, or a long speech is completely unbearable. It would mean that the image or sound image—a little girl's scream or a frightened crowd—constitute the substance of a history distinct from History, a counteranalysis of society.

Go back to the images. Do not seek in them merely the illustration, confirmation, or contradiction of another knowledge— that of written tradition. Consider images as such at the risk of using other forms of knowledge to grasp them even better. Historians have already accorded a legitimate place to sources (both written and unwritten) that have popular origins: folklore, popular arts, and traditions. We need to study film and see it in relation to the world that produces it. What is our hypothesis?—that film, image or not of reality, document or fiction, true story or pure invention, is History. Our postulate?—that what has not occurred (and even what *has* occurred)—beliefs, intentions, human imagination—is as much history as History.

The Visible and the Nonvisible[11]

Film is not considered from a semiological viewpoint here. Nor is it seen in terms of cinema history or esthetics. Film is observed not as a work of art, but as a product, an image-object, whose meanings are not solely cinematographic. Film is valuable not only because of what it reveals but also because of the sociohistorical approach that it justifies. Thus, the analyses will

29

not necessarily concern the totality of a work. They may be based on extracts, they may look for "series" or create ensembles. Nor will they be limited to the film itself. They will integrate the film into the world that surrounds it and with which it necessarily communicates.

Under these circumstances it is not enough to undertake the analysis of films or pieces of film, or shots, or themes, while taking into account (whenever necessary) the knowledge and approach of the various human sciences. It is necessary to apply these methods to each filmic element (images, sound images, images which resist sound) and to the interrelations among the components of these elements. It is necessary to analyze the film's narrative as well as its sets and language, and the relations between a film and what is extrafilmic (its author, production, public, reviews, and the state). In this way we can hope to understand not only the work but also the reality that it represents.

Moreover, this reality is not conveyed directly. Even writers are not fully the masters of words or of language. Why should it be different for the man at the camera who, in addition, involuntarily films many aspects of reality? This phenomenon is seen clearly in newsreel images. The camera may be there to shoot the arrival of "King Alexander," but if assassins turn up in the crowds, the camera records not only their movements but also the behavior of the police and the public. The resulting documents has an added richness and meaning that were not evident at the beginning. What is clear insofar as "documents" and newsreels are concerned is not any the less true of fiction where the unexpected and the involuntary can also play a great role. In a 1925 film, *Bed and Sofa* [*Tretya Meshchanskaya*, Abram Room] a couple consults a wall calendar to see when their awaited child will be born.[12] The calendar—a very common sort—bears the date of 1924. It is *already* decorated with a great portrait of Stalin. These lapses of a creator, of an ideology, or a society constitute privileged significant signs that can characterize any level of film, as well as its relationship with society. Discovering them, seeing how they agree or disagree with ideology, helps to discover what is latent behind what is apparent, helps to see the nonvisible by means of the visible. There is certainly material there for another history—one which certainly does not claim to constitute a beautiful, harmonious, and rational ensemble as does History—which can help to refine or destroy History.

The following observations deal with samples that are traditionally classified (doubtlessly in an arbitrary way) into different genres: fictional films, newsreels or documentaries, and propaganda or political films. For the sake of convenience they all have been chosen from within a relatively homogeneous corpus, contemporaneous with the birth of the U.S.S.R. (1917–26). This initial approach was necessary in order to attack the notion of the specificity of cinematographic genres. Taking this objective into account, it should be understood that this approach is not applicable to the whole field of cinema. Furthermore, this chapter is limited to a study of silent films.

The analysis of a fictional film considered apart from reality, Kuleshov's *Dura Lex* will allow us to offer an outline for a method.[13]

A *Film "Without Ideological Aims"*: Dura Lex *(1926)*

The great films of Eisenstein and Pudovkin, or Kuleshov's *The Extraordinary Adventures of Mister West in the Land of the Bolsheviks* [1924]—works of imagination and creation—touch upon themes closely associated with the birth of the U.S.S.R. and the Bolshevik regime. In their own ways these films legitimize the regime. The case is quite different when we come to *Dura Lex.* Here Kuleshov's declared aims were "to make a film which would be a work of art with an exemplary montage . . . a strong and empressive subject; to make a story film at a minimum cost—an undertaking of exceptional importance for Soviet cinema." As Lebedev notes and as Kuleshov's own words reveal, the respected master of Soviet cinema was not "concerned with revealing reality in a truthful way and did not seek to further the viewer's ideological education." Newspapers indicate that with the exception of probably one episode, the scenario essentially drew upon a Jack London story—"The Unexpected"—whose action takes place in Canada.

> A small group of gold prospectors finds a rich lode in the Klondike. The exploitation of the mine lasts the whole winter. Everything goes well. There is a lot of gold. Wine helps to shorten

the long evenings. But suddenly the well-regulated life of the gold prospectors is disturbed by a frightening event: one of the prospectors, an Irishman, Michael Dennin, shoots two members of the group at point-blank range. Overcome by greed, he wants to become the sole owner of the mine they have discovered. The Nelsens, man and wife, have time to jump upon the murderer and tie him up. Now, during the long days, husband and wife take turns guarding the bound man. Spring arrives. Melting snow cuts off the gold prospectors' shanty from the outer world. The tension of the long sleepless nights, of a life lived so close to the murderer, creates hysterical crises in the Nelsens. But their respect for the law doesn't allow them to kill Michael. Finally, the Nelsens organize an official trial of Dennin in which they themselves play the roles of judge, jury, and witnesses. Michael is condemned to be hung. The verdict is carried out by Nelsen who plays the role of the executioner this time. But when they return home, exhausted by fatigue and on the brink of madness, they find Michael on the threshold, alive, with the torn rope around his neck. The frightened Nelsens watch Michael Dennin as he goes off in the distance, into the rain and wind. [14]

A comparison between Jack London's short story and Kuleshov's work brings to light a basic difference. In "The Unexpected" the murderer is greedy and unstable, while in *Dura Lex* he is violent, of course, but also likable and pitiful. Whereas his companions are obsessed by gold and lead a feverish life, he is the only one who takes pleasure in the joys of nature, who romps about with his dog. He swims in the streams and plays the flute in his spare time. [15] Above all the film shows that his companions— who come from a higher social class than he does—keep him in an inferior position. He waits on tables, washes dishes, and performs domestic chores that the others clearly deem unworthy. In addition, although he is the one who happens to discover the lode in the film, this does not change his status. Michael Dennin does not receive thanks or tokens of esteem. Although in "The Unexpected" greed led him to crime, greed hardly appears in *Dura Lex*, which is marked instead by the revolt of a man who is constantly scoffed at and humiliated. A murderer out of dignity, Dennin collapses once he commits his crime. His face lights up only on the day when his warders invite him to their table to "celebrate a birthday." Then, as in a dream, he relates a cherished fantasy: when he becomes rich, he will go to his mother and show her that he is worthy of her love. In *Dura Lex* this drama of gratitude is also that of a citizen of inferior status. In order to condemn him, his judges take shelter behind the triple protection of English law (he is Irish), the Protestant Bible (he is Catholic), and the menace of a rifle (he is tied up). Thus, this so-called respect for legal forms is merely a parody of justice. A similar concern for forms delays the execution (executions do not take place on Sundays) and reveals the hypocrisy of a milieu, a morality, and a society. All these elements do not appear in Jack London's story where respect for legal forms is credited to the Nelsens. Conversely, in *Dura Lex* the Nelsens' reactions seem more human when, eager to avenge their friends or gripped by fear, they think of doing away with Dennin than when they restrain themselves and take it into their heads to play judge. From then on they are no longer themselves. They imitate judges, mechanically recite the legal code, blindly apply the law and, lo and behold, become transfigured, denatured, dehumanized, reduced to silhouettes.[16] Law has legitimized a crime. Other differences between the story and the film help to understand the way Kuleshov proceeds. In "The Unexpected" the neighboring Indian community soon learns of Dennin's crime when by chance, Negook, one of its members, enters the cabin and sees the cadavers and blood. Appearances are against the Nelsens because Dennin is tied up. In order that nothing seems equivocal and that Dennin really seems to have been fairly judged, his trial takes place in public. The Indians watch it and even if they do not understand the procedure, the issue is clear because Dennin recounts and re-enacts his crime. *Dura Lex* has nothing of that. The trial takes place behind closed doors. Dennin can hardly defend himself. Thus, while Jack London glorified the Edith Nelsen who wants to try Dennin and respect the law, Kuleshov shows that the so-called respect for law is merely a parody that is worse than violence. Certain procedures are so revolting that the judges themselves are gripped by delirium. As if in a nightmare, after the execution the Nelsens see Dennin alive once more—a scene not found in Jack London.

Can such additions, omissions, modifications, and reversals

be attributed merely to the "genius" of the artist? Do they not have another meaning? One that is revealed by a lapse of the filmmaker? Although he is careful to situate the action on British soil down to the smallest details, he organizes the great birthday celebration *à la russe*.[17] From then on it becomes clear that the complete reversal of meanings created by Kuleshov is not accidental. Russia—the U.S.S.R. of the first Stalinist trials—lies hidden behind the mask of Canada.[18]

From then on it becomes understandable why the film received such a lukewarm welcome from the "critics." Although *Pravda* declared that it saw an attack against bourgeois justice in *Dura Lex*, the press remained reserved deciding the portrayal was "unconvincing." However, it did not offer any explicit reason for this judgment except that the work was "overly dominated by psychological motives." This reason makes sense only in relation to Jack London's story. Edith is his heroine, and his aim is to analyze the behavior of a young bourgeois woman faced with the risks and unexpected elements in life. But this explanation is irrelevant where the film is concerned. *Pravda* also felt that *Dura Lex* was "a projectile launched in a futile path." However, since the *Pravda* critic also wrote that the film dealt with a "trial of bourgeois justice and religious practices" and since 1926 marked the height of the campaign against religion, his negative verdict might seem surprising. But this verdict becomes more understandable if the film is seen as an attack against any law, any procedure, any justice—be it popular or even Soviet. While the mouthing of the code and law on the part of the Nelsens, those would-be judges, constitutes on the surface a parody of English justice, Soviet authorities perceived it as a criticism of their own judiciary practices which, in effect, were denounced by this work by means of a "Canadian adventure."

Was the author entirely conscious of this? Was he able to acknowledge it? Was official criticism able or willing to see clearly and admit what it had seen? We are faced with a double censorship which transcribes a reality that remains nonvisible at the level of film, written texts, and evidence. But it is a zone of reality, nonetheless, that images help to discover, define, and demarcate.

Thus, starting from the ostensible content of this "Western," the analysis of images and the criticism of sources have allowed us to spot the film's latent content. *Russia is hidden behind Canada* and victims of repression behind Dennin's trial. This analysis also allowed us to discover a *zone of nonvisible reality*. Critics in this Soviet society hid from themselves the true reasons for their attitudes (agreement/disagreement) vis-à-vis the film. The filmmaker transposed (consciously/unconsciously) a story, totally reversing its key point (without saying it, without anyone wanting to see it). Jack London's signature offered Kuleshov an ultimate reassurance since a 1906 work by London—"Why I Am a Socialist"—had been widely diffused by the Bolsheviks the preceding year.[19]

The above procedure can be seen through the diagram opposite which, with adjustments, can be applied to newsreels or political films.

Comparing the First Soviet and Anti-Soviet Propaganda Films

We will present both films (*Congestion* [Soviet] and *Days of Terror at Kiev* [German, 1918]), their scenarios (a), and aspects of the mise-en-scène (b). Then we will compare them. This comparison will reveal some aspects of the mentality—unsaid and non-explicit—of the revolutionary era.

1. (a) *Congestion* [*Uplotnenive*], one of the first films of the Soviet regime, made in 1918 by Panteleyev, was scripted by Minister of Culture Anatoli Lunacharsky. In his own words, and according to critics of that era, the film "showed the necessity for the fusion of the proletariat and intellectual classes." Here is a synopsis of it.

> One year after the success of the great October Revolution, an eminent professor in Petrograd is giving chemistry courses. Although his ideas were by no means shared by all the professors, he was like many intellectuals with advanced ideas who remained detached from the Revolution from the very first, believing, in the words of one of his students, that "science must always remain removed from politics." In point of fact, he leads the agitation

society + ideology			
search for			
signs			
fiction			
apparent		latent	zone of nonvisible
content		content	(social) reality
image of reality			
society + ideology			

against the Bolsheviks. The professor's oldest son is also an enemy of the Revolution. The youngest, a high-school student, remains at the crossroads. A worker and his daughter are brought to live in the professor's apartment because of the humidity in the basement where they were living. Members of the professor's family behave in various ways vis-à-vis the new tenants. But before long the animosity of the professor's wife and his young son disappears. Factory workers begin to frequent the apartment of the professor, who starts giving courses for the people in a workers' club. The professor's son falls in love with the worker's daughter and they unite their destinies.

(b) Certain features of the film were not noticed when it came out. The neighborhood delegate comes to announce the good news to the worker. In his pocket he has a mandate to requisition the professor's apartment on the second floor. The worker feels embarrassed. He does not dare dirty the vestibule's luxurious carpet. The delegate pushes him, saying, "it's your right."[20] Once on the steps the worker hesitates again. The delegate rings the bell for him, bullies him, spits conspicuously into the elevator shaft. The requisition papers in his hand, the worker is still reluctant to enter the apartment. The delegate bullies him and speaks to him as if to an inferior: "You don't need to hesitate; it's your right." Whereas the sight of the requisition causes his wife to faint, the professor welcomes the tenants very graciously. He offers them a sort of cohabitation. "Not cohabitation, but sharing," demands the delegate. Nevertheless, the worker and his daughter are gradually treated as boarders. But while the reticent young girl remains in her room, her father no longer withdraws into his assigned room where he awkwardly had something to eat the first day. He takes his meals at the common table and his daughter eventually joins him. Both of them watch the two sons quarrel violently over the Revolution and bolshevism, quarrels which neither the worker nor his daughter seems to understand. Following an argument, a policeman comes to arrest the older son who is hostile to the Bolsheviks and who the inspectors identify by his young officer's uniform. They don't even question him. The younger son falls in love with the young girl while the old worker introduces the professor to his club, which is named after Karl Liebknecht. The professor is received as a friend and gives chemistry lessons that are like magical seances for these rough workers. The workers do not know how to express their gratitude to the professor, who becomes their advisor and brother. But the civil war goes on, and it is necessary to fight. The professor and his younger son are with the Reds. The elder son, who went over to the side of the Whites after he was freed by the police, is killed in battle.

2. The director of the first anti-Soviet film, *Days of Terror at Kiev*, is unknown.[21] The film was made in 1918 in Kiev under the aegis of the German authorities who were protecting the White Russian general Pavel Petrovich Skoropadski. The titles

are in German and French. The struggle against the Bolsheviks has turned the national enemy into an ally, and the French—at whom the film was also aimed—have landed troops not far away, at Odessa.

(a) The Reds have assumed power at Kiev. Violence and crime are the law. Honorable citizens have been cleared out and their dwellings occupied. The film traces the tragedy of one of these petit bourgeois families. The father has lost his job. He and his wife have been expelled from their apartment by their former valet "who fulfills important functions with the Bolsheviks." Their daughter, "who works with the Bolsheviks," wants to help and protect them. But the parents refuse her money, which is "earned by unworthy means." Soon the father is sent "to forced labor." With the help of a comrade also won over by the Bolsheviks, his daughter attempts to organize his escape abroad. But the father, the mother, and the friend are victims of a plot instigated by the former valet. They are discovered, arrested, and shot.

(b) Certain elements in the scenario and its mise-en-scène emphasize the general thrust of this synopsis. Promiscuity and turpitude reign among the Bolsheviks and "it is these people who govern." They throw down the master's chauffeur, thrash him, take his belongings, strip him, and take his automobile for themselves. At the police station, a smoke-filled den flooded by alcohol, inspectors are arrogant with the citizens, spineless with superiors. Sweat oozes everywhere. At the work camp the man in charge is a converted bourgeois who is that much more unyielding with his victims. This sadist "has no respect for white hair, nor for patriots." The other young converted bourgeois (the daughter's friend) is a criminal. He informs the Bolsheviks about his friend's plan. We see him deteriorate once he comes into contact with the Bolsheviks.

In the bourgeois group, on the contrary, order, honesty, and rectitude reign. When the young hoodlums move in, seat themselves at table, and finish the father's meal, the old man keeps his dignity. This drama puts to the test his wife, who faints. After having cursed her daughter, she embraces her when the latter wants to help her parents. Right up to the end she shows that she is a good mother.

3. A comparison of these two political films, made within months of each other, one by the Whites and the other by the Reds, leads us to observe that despite opposing goals they have almost the same thematic line.

—They raise the problem of relations between the conquerers of October and the petite bourgeoisie.

—Their goal is to show that cohabitation or the fusion of classes is impossible/possible.

—The principal traumatic element is being expelled from or being forced to share a bourgeois apartment. The mother is more sensitive to this then the rest of the family. Allegorically, the victims live underground: some before October (in the Bolshevik film), others after October (in the anti-Bolshevik film).

—The fact of the Revolution creates political conflicts that burst out in the family cell and dissolve it.

—Although the final sequence is tragic, the actual tragic scenes are omitted. We see neither the death of the older son (who is hostile to the Bolsheviks) in *Congestion*, nor how the young girl of *Days of Terror at Kiev* conforms to the new regime.

Other equivalences and similarities go beyond the conscious or unconscious desire of the scriptwriters.

—In both films a romance inspires the way the classes are brought together. Nonetheless, there is a difference. In *Days of Terror at Kiev* the initiative comes from the young girl who has done something improper in "leaving" home. In *Congestion* it is the younger son "who falls in love"; the young female worker maintains a very reserved attitude that reveals her good upbringing. Thus, we have two films with opposite endings that both, however, define good or evil starting from the same sign, a young girl's behavior. While this is hardly surprising in a film defending traditional moral principles, it is surprising when one knows the views set forth by Lunacharsky on women's emancipation. In his eyes does emancipation only apply to women of the intelligentsia, while tradition is still the "best morality" for the people?

—In neither film are the activists workers.

—In *Congestion* the neighborhood delegate wearing a leather vest makes all the decisions and the worker obeys. In *Days of Terror at Kiev* the Bolsheviks are soldiers, sailors, a valet, some petit bourgeois—not workers. When the author wants to castigate "the regime" he shows the misdeeds of the "rabble," inserts the title "and they govern" followed by a newsreel shot showing not the workers but an assembly of soldiers.

We see that these two films completely omit any mention of the great measures traditionally attributed to the Bolshevik regime, such as the decree concerning peace. This is true for many other films of these years, if not for those by the Whites (because many filmmakers were emigrating), at least for those of the Soviets. It was still several years before the glorification of the great accomplishments of October would fill the screen.

The explanation for this delay is found, above all, in the real thrust of the decrees of 1918. The peace decree? The "imperialist" war was succeeded first by civil war, then by the struggle against foreign intervention. The land decree? In 1918 no one had forgotten that most of the peasants took over the land *by themselves*, before October legitimized and enlarged the expropriation measures. Nor could the Whites raise the issue of factory self-control since what they baptized as worker control signaled the end of factory committees. Thus, we see that all these censored topics singularly limited the field of political film.[22] In the general stagnancy it was clear that the Bolshevik party needed the bourgeoisie if it was to regenerate the economy. It knew this and so did the Whites. Thus, the protagonists focus their propaganda on the problems that were really the most traumatic for the floating mass of the petite bourgeoisie: the loss of one's hearth, the appropriation of *consumer* goods, the crossing of social lines. At this time, the die not yet cast, the Whites tried to stem the tide by frightening this petite bourgeoisie. In order to win the petite bourgeoisie over, the Reds sought to seduce it.

In other respects the two films show the lower classes taking over management. Workers or not, the men and women who make decisions do not belong to the former ruling strata. The way they dress, eat, and behave shows the difference; there is a visible and measurable gap. This situation was to change. From the 1920s on, documents and films reveal that it fell to the members of the old intelligentsia to take their turn at being transformed into bureaucrats.

Analysis of Newsreels Documenting the Petrograd Street
Demonstrations of February–October, 1917

Seeking special rather than everyday events, the film-hound films only nonreconstructed reality. But this does not enable him to get to the bottom of problems because societal forces— interacting with the needs of his employers as well as customs— limit the field of his activities.

But even if it is circumscribed, the richness of the newsreel document—chosen, reduced, cut, and edited—remains irreplaceable. This can be measured by very banal examples of newsreels about a street demonstration.[23]

Documentation here is relatively plentiful. Moreover, since the revolutionary movement lasted several months and processions often followed the same path—along the Liteiny and Nevsky Prospect and toward Taurido Palace—Russian, English, and French cameramen were able to locate good angles for shooting.[24] These circumstances account for the existence of a real "series" of documents on the street demonstrations. These shots are easily situated chronologically thanks to the inscriptions written on banners, often shot frontally or from a three-quarters view. Thus, some read: "Down with the Old Regime," "Long Live the Democratic Republic," "Long Live the Constituent Assembly," "Without Equal Rights for Women, No Democracy," and "Equal and Direct Suffrage for All." When these key words are shown together, it is clear that the demonstrations took place at the beginning of the Revolution. Other scenes of demonstrators date undeniably from the April crisis. As a matter of fact, the banners read: "Peace without Annexations or Revenues" and "Down with the Policy of Aggression." Those of their opponents read "War until Victory." The June 18 procession was filmed extensively: "Down with the Six Capitalist Ministers," "Land and Liberty," "Down with the Duma." Later on we find demonstrators once again carrying the same slogans. The most frequent are "War until Victory," "General Peace," and "Peace without Annexations or Revenues."

Certain observations can be made concerning these shots. In March, as those leading the procession moved along, shopkeepers and rubbernecks in the petit bourgeois neighborhoods in the center of the city applauded and before long were indistinguishable from the demonstrators—they had merged with the procession. Women were numerous. In April and May the processions were more disciplined and moved ahead with flags and banners. Rubbernecks, shopkeepers, and passers-by looked at or accompanied the demonstrators but did not leave the sidewalk. They did not merge with them. In June and during the summer the mass of demonstrators was less thick. The public went about its business and paid little attention to the pacifist parades, while a double police force, with a cordon of troops, guarded the safety of the demonstration.

Thus, images furnish a kind of time frame marking relations between the demonstrators and the petite bourgeoisie in the center of the capital: first unity, then sympathy or indifference, and finally fear or hostility. They do not show anything very new as far as traditional history is concerned. But they do give us an immediate sense of the movement of the Revolution, from the extraordinary tumult of the February days to the demonstrations that were joyous at first and then, as the months progressed, calm and then tense and disillusioned.

However, a second reading brings a new fact to light. Hardly any workers are seen among all these demonstrators. The overwhelming majority is composed of soldiers. Among the civilians, women are dominant and, among them, feminist processions rather than delegations of female workers. National delegations (Bunds, Dashnaks, and so forth) are also numerous. All this is verified by fiction. In Eisenstein's *October* [*Oktyabre (Ten Days that Shook the World)* 1928], the demonstrator who raises the flag over the statute in February is a woman. The crowd that follows brandishes scythes and rifles but not hammers. These scythes and rifles are seen twice. Workers do not appear before the July demonstrations and do not prepare for the October uprising. In fact iconography confirms that between February and October, aside from May 1 and July 3, worker participation in demonstrations and processions was very minor.

This puts into question a firmly rooted tradition concerning "mass demonstrations of workers and soldiers." Encouraged to verify this by the newsreels, we see that between February and October, the activists who burst into the seat of the Bolshevik party in order to make it take charge of the April, June, and July demonstrations were never workers but really soldiers. In truth, if the workers did not demonstrate in the center of the city, it was simply because, for the most part, they were occupying and managing the factories. A fictional film by Pudovkin shows this other side of the issue: *The End of St. Petersburg* [*Konyets Sankkt-Peterburga* 1927] makes it clear that before February workers met in their homes. The factory was seen as a hostile fortress where they went to work and from which they recovered in the evening. At other hours of the day or night everything surrounding it was empty. However, between February and October homes were left empty because life moved to the factory that became, along with its neighboring streets, a buzzing city and a home to the laborers.

The traditional silence concerning this aspect of the revolutionary movement is explicable. For Bolshevik historiography to note the rarity of workers in the street demonstrations and to explain this by noting that workers were busy occupying factories would be tantamount to an admission that the measures taken later on to put an end to worker management went against a general consensus. Besides, Marxist tradition could not attribute the success of the great street demonstrations of April and June to these soldiers who were defined—by dogma and law—as "peasants in uniform."[25] Recognizing even the partial avant-garde political role of these "peasant-soldiers" rather than the workers would thus have a double significance: not only would it invalidate actions taken by the Bolsheviks later on, but it would place into question the dogma legitimizing their authority.

These documents also reveal the extraordinary popularity of the uprising that began in February, the conscious awakening that accompanied it, and the unalloyed joy at being rid of the aristocracy. Compared to pre-1917 documents, these shots concerning the demonstrations concretely reveal how the city gradually changed hands, changes signaling the social upheaval that subtended these political demonstrations. Given the people's seizure of power, October can be seen as a legitimization, not as a coup d'état or a historical accident.

These three examples, chosen in Russia, show that any film—whatever it may be—is always submerged by its content. Behind the reality that is represented, it always allows us to reach a historical zone which, up until then, remained hidden, nongraspable, and nonvisible. With *Dura Lex* we can spot the omissions of artists and official critics that reveal the nonexplicit prohibitions at work at the beginning of the Terror. The newsreels have revealed the popularity of October and have also stripped the historical tradition of certain false assumptions. But by the implications underlying their understanding of events, these newsreels also mask a part of political and social reality. The comparison between the two propaganda films has shown the gap that can exist between historical reality seized at the level of lived experience and the way we view it later on. It also shows how a ruling class was banished from History.

Taken together, these films have, to a certain degree, demonstrated the mechanism of rational history. Analyzing them has helped us to better grasp the relation between society and its rulers. This is not to say that the rational vision of history is not operational, but only to remind us that in order to let nothing escape, the analysis must not favor any single approach, thereby becoming totalitarian.

(1971)

NOTES

1. To use Michel Foucault's expression in *L'Archéologie du savoir* (Paris: Gallimard, 1969), pp. 14–15.
2. See, for example, Georges Lefebvre, *La Naissance de l'historiographie moderne* (Paris: Flammarion, 1971); J. Ehrard and G. Palmade, *L'Histoire* (Paris: Colin, 1965); and A. G. Widgery, *Les Grandes doctrines de L'Histoire* (Paris: Gallimard, 1965). On the historian's discourses, see Roland Barthes, "Le discours de l'Histoire," *Social Science, Information sur les sciences sociales* (August, 1967), 65–77.
3. For the origins of historiography and Etienne Pasquier, see G. Huppert, "Naissance de l'Histoire en France: les 'Récherches d'Etienne Pasquier,' " *Annales* (E.S.C.), 1 (1968), 69–106.
4. Quoted in Pierra Nora, "Ernest Lavisse, son rôle dans la formation du sentiment national," *Revue historique* (1962), 73–102.
5. [Translator's note: Ferro is referring here to an early Lumière film "L'Arivée du train à la Ciotat."]

44

Counteranalysis of Society?

6. B. Edelman, "De la nature des oeuvres d'art d'après la jurispru-
dence," *Recueil Dalloz Sirey* (1969), 61–70.
7. Two counter societies—the Nazis and the Soviets—include the
cameraman's name in the credits of newsreels.
8. F. Furet's "Sur quelques problèmes posés par le développement de
l'Histoire quantitative," *Social Science, Information sur les sciences sociales*
(1968), 71–83. Also Furet's "Histoire quantitative et fait historique," *Annales*
(E.S.C.) 1 (1971), 63–76.
9. Concerning these problems cf. Jean-Patrick Lebel's *Cinéma et
idéologie* (Paris: Editions de la Nouvelle Critique/Editions sociales, 1971), p.
230.
10. Let us remember the analysis of Edgar Morin in *Le Cinéma et
l'homme imaginaire* (Paris: Editions de Minuit, 1956), p. 250. Reprinted by
Gonthier.
11. On Soviet cinema see the work and bibliography of Jay Leyda, *Kino:
A History of the Russian and Soviet Film* (London, New York: Macmillan,
1960), p. 490. We have also used works by Georges Sadoul, Maurice Bardèche,
Jean Mitry, and, by Christian Metz, "Les propositions méthodologiques pour
l'analyse du film," *Social Science, Information sur les sciences sociales* (August,
1968), 107–21. We also thank A. Akoun, M.-F. Briselance, A. Goldmann, A.
Margarido, H. Grigoriadou-Cabagnols, B. Rolland, G. Fihman, and C.
Ezyckman, who have been kind enough to read this text and help us to improve
it.
12. [Translator's note: Ferro appears mistaken here. Both Lebedev in *Il
cinema muto sovietico* (Turin: Einaudi, 1962) and Leyda in *Kino* list the film's
date as 1927.]
13. On Kuleshov and *Dura Lex* see "Russie: années 20," *Cahiers du
cinéma* (March–June, 1970).
14. The text of this synopsis, like those following, was taken from a
translation of Lebedev published in *Le film muet soviétique* (Catalogue de la
cinémathèque de Bruxelles, n.d.)
15. As M.-F. Briselance has observed.
16. In the shots filmed against the light (as L. Grigoriadou-Cabgnols has
observed).
17. Cf. Leyda, *Kino*, p. 213.
18. Aside from the measures taken against the Whites and their partisans, the trial of the Socialist Revolutionaries took place in May, 1922; that of
the left-wing Socialist Revolutionaries, the artisans of October, in 1921, like
that of the Mensheviks. The first trial with a written confession dates from the
end of 1924. Up to that time a real procedure was followed. All the same it was
readily violated by the tribunal. The most frequent of these violations was that
the defense was forbidden to produce witnesses. Cf. Leonard Schapiro, *The
Origin of the Communist Autocracy of Political Opposition in the Soviet State:
First Phase, 1917–1922* (Cambridge: Harvard University Press, 1955).
19. "Pocemu ja socialistom?" (Leningrad, 1925).
20. The quotation marks correspond to the titles.
21. A German propaganda film shot at Kiev in 1919 with Russian actors.
The film is preceded by a montage of documents entitled "Bolshevik Atrocities"
("Die Bolschewisten breuel"). Running time is ten minutes. *National Film
Archive Catalogue* (London, n.d.), part II, no. 163.

45

22. Cf. Leyda, *Kino,* chapter 7.

23. An inventory of such footage is in preparation. A catalogue of footage found in the U.S.S.R. is found in N. P. Abramov and V. P. Mikhailov, eds., *Kiono i foto dokumenty po istorii velikogo Oktjabrja, 1910–1920* (Moscow: Izd-vo Akademii nauk, 1958), p. 354.

24. Except for May 1. Besides, on that day the demonstrations did not take place on the Liteiny and Nevsky Prospects but on the Field of Mars Square.

25. Wrongly, as I have shown in "Le soldat russe: indiscipline, patriotisme, pacifisme, et révolution," *Annales, XXVI,* 1 (Jan.–Feb., 1971), 14–139.

CHAPTER 2

Fiction and Reality in the Cinema:
A Strike in Old Russia

It is easy to think that film is not suited to represent past reality and that at best its testimony is valuable only for the present; or that, aside from documents and newsreels, the reality it offers is no more real than the novel's.

I think that this is not true and that, paradoxically, the only films that do not manage to surpass film's testimony concerning the present are films about the past: historical reconstructions. Let us take another look at masterpieces such as *Alexander Nevsky* or *Andrei Rubylov* [Tarkovsky, 1966]. Their reproduction of the past is exemplary. To understand medieval Russia, in fact, one has to mentally banish the obsessive images offered by these reconstructions. In this sense *Rubylov* and *Nevsky* are two extraordinary object films. However, they are nothing more than that, a bit the way the "histories" of Kovaleski or Kljusevski are object books. The past brought to life in them is only a mediated past, the Soviet Union as its rulers wanted it to be in 1938 and the Soviet Union seen by its opponents in 1970. And it is brought to life through the choice of themes, the tastes of an era, production necessities, the strength of the writing, and the creator's omissions. Clearly, this is where the true historical reality of these films is found, not in their representations of the past.

Conversely, films where the action is contemporaneous with the film's realization are not merely witnesses of the imaginary universe of that era. Since they involve elements that reach beyond the immediate moment, they transmit to us the real image of the past. This characteristic obviously marks certain documents of reality. How can we date these Tiflis streets filmed in 1908?—or this scene of wheat threshing shot in 1912? The paradox is that this observation is even more valid for fictional films. Their image of reality can be as true as a document's. The technique of making Russian boots in *Patriots* [*Okraina*, Boris Barnet, 1933] or the bustle of a leather market in *Storm over Asia* [*Potomok Chingis-Khan*, Pudovkin, 1928] are examples that could be easily multiplied if we wanted to use films to create an imaginary museum of the Russian past. Fiction can delve into the analysis of the way past eras functioned economically and can study their mentality. It is hard to conceive of a more authentic testimony about marriage in ancient Russia than the first sequences of Olga Preobrazhenskaya's film *Women of Ryazan* [*Babi ryazanskye*, 1927]. The choice of the groom, the financial transactions, dowry calculations, the preparation of the young bride, and the nuptial ceremony all constitute an extraordinary bit of social history. Furthermore, in these sequences each shot is a tableau that historical criticism could analyze in detail. This is a grazing ground which has been neglected for too long.

The problem is a methodological one that involves detecting reality by means of fiction and the imaginary. This is what I tried to do in Chapter 1. We also saw that newsreels, fictional films, and propaganda films constitute materials for the historian. The aim of the following observations concerning *Strike* [*Stachka*, Eisenstein, 1925] and a strike in *Mother* [*Mat*, Pudovkin, 1926] is to show that, through their descriptions of the imaginary strikes of their contemporaries, Pudovkin and Einsenstein brought as much to history as History. The strike constitutes but one episode in Pudovkin's film. It is the very heart of Einsenstein's work. Let us look at the scenario of Eisenstein's six-act "ciné-play" *Strike*.

In one of the greatest factories of Czarist Russia, all is outwardly calm. The workers toil and the bourgeoisie enjoys life. But the factory foreman notices a secret emotion among the workers. He lets the management know about this and the management tells the police. Spys penetrate into all the chinks of the factory and the workers' town. Nonetheless, the committee of the Russian Worker Social Democrat party launches proclamations calling for a struggle. The suicide of a worker who was unjustly accused provokes the strike. Workers leave the factory. Machines stop. A meeting is organized in the woods. Learning of the bosses' refusal to satisfy the workers' demands, the committee decides to continue the strike. The police have the wine warehouse set afire in the belief that the workers will loot it and thus provoke repressions. But this plan fails. Upon the order of the chief of police, firemen aim their hoses at the workers in order to disperse them. Those responsible are arrested. But the strike does not stop. Once more the workers go out into the streets. And then a bloody massacre begins. Dozens and dozens of workers are massacred, just as the miners of Lenski and the workers of Jaroslavl' and other industrial cities of Russia fell by the thousands.

Let us leave to one side visible reality, the film's sets and exteriors: isbas and buildings of old Russia, workshop organization, and factory structure. Let us look only at social functioning. The workers lack solidarity. Their divisions reflect antagonisms that are not ideological (Bolshevik/Menshevik, Marxist/populist) but are linked to the way different age groups function in the factory. It is significant that the unity of the working class is represented by a stationary shot of three generations of workers. The dissension always comes from the oldest. They break the strike in Pudovkin's *Mother* and act as double agents or agents provocateurs in *Strike*. Those who inspire the workers' movement are always young—their children are six or seven years old at the most. Clearly, these workers have recently come from the countryside. Happy and relaxed, they get their bearings and fulfill themselves there; it is there that they were born, enjoy themselves, play, love, and die. Conversely, the stool pigeons and scabs are city people. Their realm is that of the cabaret and the sidewalk. That is where they feel at ease and win their battles.

The second group of workers opposed to the strikers includes the foremen whose hesitations, at times, express their ambiguous status in the factory. The other populist elements hostile to the strikers within and without the factory—the doorman, stokers (who set off the sirens), firemen ("the bastards, they aim their nozzles against their brothers"), and servants—are workers who have been given some authority, if not privileges. They open or close doors, watch over workmen, set everyone to work, approach the boss, assure the safety of whoever needs it.

The working class lives in a ghetto. It is territorially and socially isolated, and even within the ghetto neighbors are generally indifferent, if not hostile, to the workers' aspirations. People believe it is wrong to strike, not because it would mean that parents could no longer feed their children ("let the children work"), but because the refusal to work is likened to a mutiny. Not working is not fulfilling one's duty; it is disobeying. The factory is also likened to prison barracks where one must "behave well" because no one is there without reason. Besides, asking for raises and formulating demands is, in the words of an owner, "politicking." This view prevails among the older people. Their life of submission only makes sense if it corresponds to the law. The old people of *Mother* have confidence in the equity of officers, judges, and the state. The son's condemnation is what makes his mother become aware that she has been a dupe and she writes "gde pravda," which means both "where is justice?" and "where is truth?"

The social distance between them excludes any direct contact between the workers and the ruling classes. Although the bosses are less anonymous than bureaucrats, they still communicate with the inferior class only through subaltern intermediaries—personnel heads, police chiefs, or militia officers. Their indifference to the fate of the workers is absolute. In the eyes of these educated, delicate, and sensitive people, the judge's new mare [*Mother*] and the shareholders automatic bar [*Strike*] are more interesting than the list of demands made by the strikers or the deportation of the strikers to Siberia. Even the principal lawyer, who is working to save the prisoners from the death penalty, could not come to the hearing because "he was detained by his affairs." Furthermore, all these "well-raised" people are in complicity with each other—the lawyer with the judge, the manager with the general, and, as we see in *Battleship Potemkin*, the doctor with the officer.

We can observe that women are always linked to climactic situations. They transmit the order to strike, either encourage or discourage the others to go ahead with it, and provoke recourse to violence ("Hit him," they yell in *October* and *Strike*; the mother screams "Help, comrades!" in *Strike*). Their role is always central, determining, presaging death or bloodshed.

The launching of the strike and the repression do not come from inexorable elements built into the process of cause and effect. In *Strike*, although the workers are discontented and tracts are distributed, nothing happens. The strike, which is widespread, spontaneous, and instantaneous, bursts out because a worker—in despair because he was falsely accused of having stolen a micrometer—has committed suicide. The foreman who accused him is shoved, beaten, and then ridiculed. He is not considered responsible for his foul deed. It is the system that is responsible for everything, and it is because of that that the strike is a general one. The accusation was not necessary for the system to function well, but it did reveal its human side. Like the worms that crawl over the meat in *Battleship Potemkin* (worms the doctor wants to ignore), it traumatizes the victims, enabling them to see the extent of the scorn directed at them.

Like the strike, the repression also breaks out in an irrational fashion that is apparently unrelated to either the way the system functions or the oppressors' needs. The demands of the workers have been rejected. Although the workers have foiled the attempt to provoke them, they demonstrated and were dispersed by the police. The incident could have stopped there. But a child happens to stray under the hooves of a mounted policeman and when his mother runs to save her little one, the policeman whips her. She calls, "Help, comrades!" and, instantaneously, the fight erupts which leads to the general massacre of the workers. The inexorability of violence, the cruelty of the state's servants, and the indifference of well-educated people are all necessary parts of the system revealed by this apparently irrational process.

Pudovkin's *Mother* provides another instance where the process of launching the strike does not correspond merely to salary demands. The word to strike, which comes from the outside, is not analyzed but rather executed. It emanates from a mysterious and distant staff officer whose authority is sufficiently accepted that his decisions are not questioned. As in *Strike* each person must decide the extent of his or her own commitment and whether to further or interrupt the momentum. In *Mother* the order to strike is transmitted by a young girl who is clearly from the intelligentsia; through a lapse of the author, she is not a Social Democrat but a populist since she brings weapons to the workers. In this fashion Pudovkin correctly restores to the people their inspirational role. Eisenstein never introduces Bolshevik leaders into his films. It is the nonfilmic elements (that are in some sense outside the film) such as the opening and closing titles that recall the party's words and acts. A similar lapse is also found in *October*. Thus at every level Einsenstein valorizes spontaneity as opposed to organization.

Eisenstein's *Strike* is a condensation or a digest of these great strikes illustrating the proletariat's struggle in pre–1917 Russia. But it is more than that, for it can also be seen as a kind of model of industrial society once it arrives at that stage of its development which is shaped by the presence of demands, crises, strikes, provocation, and repression. This model also raises problems concerning social functioning and the spontaneity and organization of what is inevitable or irrational in the revolutionary process.

(1972)

CHAPTER 3

Stalinist Ideology Seen through *CHAPAYEV*

To further my aim of sketching out a general methodology concerning the analysis of fictional films, I have chosen *Chapayev* [Sergei and Georgy Vasiliev, 1934] as an example.[1] We will examine the film's reception vis-à-vis its author's intentions. Then, starting with its *découpage* and some elements of its realization, we will compare the film's explicit content with the latent ideology of its text and images.

Chapayev offers something very special. Upon its release the film was greeted by a front page editorial in *Pravda* that saw it as an example worthy of inspiring Soviet filmmakers. "We do not ask for a new *Chapayev* every day," another leader modestly wrote several weeks later. Before long, for the first time since 1917, *Pravda* devoted an entire page to Soviet cinema in which the Vasilievs were given an important place. The reasons for this enthusiasm were clearly shown in an editorial of November 21, 1934, which noted that this film "showed what the party's organizing role was, how a link had been established between the party and the masses, and how the party had organized and disciplined spontaneity."

53

Communist parties abroad echoed these sentiments. It is significant that in Madrid the Republican government ensured the film's distribution in the midst of the Civil War. Cinematographic newsreels testify to the poster campaign advertising the Vasilievs' work. The reasons for this are readily understandable. *Chapayev* presents the 1918–19 Civil War. The Reds are present as a model, but the film shows the need for centralization at a time when in Spain this issue was at the heart of the conflict between Communists and anarchists. *Chapayev* shows that heros make mistakes, that spontaneity leads to errors, and that individuals die. On the other hand, the party sees correctly, never makes mistakes, and never dies.

Let us look at an outline of the film as well as a Soviet critic's commentary from 1934. *Chapayev* takes place in 1919 during the Civil War. Chapayev is leading a victorious but somewhat disorganized campaign against the Whites. To hold him in check and educate him politically, the party sends Furmanov to Chapayev as political commissar. Furmanov is to share the divisional command with him. The film traces the relations between the two men as well as the general conditions surrounding the struggle against the Whites. The Soviet critic's thoughts on *Chapayev* are:

> The film opens with an episode showing Chapayev's retreat before the thrust of the White Guards who in 1918 were active on the Volga. Chapayev's troops, composed of heterogeneous elements, offer little resistance: clearly it seems that we are not yet dealing with the Red Army, but simply with one of the spontaneous detachments of partisans that later on were to supply it with numerous recruits. But here is Chapayev who appears amidst this rout. He stops those who are fleeing and leads them back to the attack. He himself leads the battle, aiming the machine gun. And the viewer is immediately taken by the ardent temperament of this legendary chief who has come from the ranks of poor peasants. Upon seeing him, his soldiers stop, turn victoriously against the enemy and crush it. Retreat is transformed into victory. Chapeyev thanks his companions for their bravery and force. Forthwith, however, he becomes the stern educator that every true popular chief must be. He demands that everyone who has thrown away or lost his gun in the retreat find it and present it to him. All hunt

for their guns, some even diving into the river. In the midst of all this, Chapayev's division is reinforced by a detachment of workers from Ivancvo-Voznesensk, led by Furmanov who must now fulfill the functions of political commissar. From this moment on complex relations are established between the two men.

Furmanov understands the difficulty of the task that has fallen to him: he must re-educate the partisans in order to turn them into conscious Red soldiers and he must help their improvised and talented leader become a commander of the regular Red Army. What Bolshevik tenacity, what patience, tact, and courage will be necessary to achieve this aim! With an astonishing penetration, the film shows us this process of political re-education that takes place not on school benches, but in the feverish and tense atmosphere of a divisional staff headquarters. Gradually, Furmanov wins a victory for the Bolshevik ideological leadership, at the same time consolidating his authority in the eyes of the combatants.

But is not the most arduous side of Furmanov's task the re-education of Chapayev himself? At their first meeting Chapayev does not want to allow the newly appointed commissar to intrude into his division. He does not want to defer to anyone. Chapayev takes advantage of the first military conference that brings them together on the eve of a battle to test the commissar's skills and character by asking him his opinion about the plan of operations. Perhaps he would have enjoyed mischieviously making fun of the commissar if the latter had talked and revealed his ignorance of the military art. But Furmanov does not hide the fact that he asks only to learn about this art from Chapayev as he calmly continues to study the commander, as well as his soldiers and milieu.

Before long we witness a scene that reveals other character traits of Chapayev. When the brigade commander, Yelan, receives a wound in his hand, he is welcomed by these cutting words of Chapayev: "Wounded! That's an imbecile for you!" Completely embarrassed, Yelan answers: "Bullets don't choose." "It's up to you to choose," yells Chapayev, "you need gumption." And in front of the commissar, in the witty form of a lesson concerning concrete things, he shows the brigade commander how he should direct the battle. Here Chapayev appears in a somewhat unexpected light.

Despite his natural military talent, his military strategy does not depend upon chance. He demands that the battle be directed in a deliberate way: "You need gumption!" And in this way a second essential trait of Chapayev's character surfaces: the need for reason, organization, discipline.

Nothing is more remarkable than a scene—in which we get to know Chapayev better—where Furmanov and Chapayev discuss Alexander of Macedonia. Chapayev thought that he knew about military history, but it so happens that he has not even heard about the great Macedonian. Furmanov tries to comfort him by telling him that Alexander the Great has been dead a long time and that many people know nothing about him. Chapayev isn't satisfied with this response. He is deeply imbued with the feeling of dignity characterizing workers who have broken the bonds of oppression. "You know it," he answers, "so I should know it too." His thirst for knowledge is as ardent as his military activity. You need only look at his face for an instant to feel all the impetuosity and all the vitality of the spirit at work behind his large brow where thought is inseparable from action.

Beginning with his first meeting with Furmanov, he clearly realizes deep down that many things could be improved as far as his division and its partisan spirit are concerned. He concludes from this that he does not know enough, and he expresses the desire to educate himself at Furmanov's side. Thus Chapayev reveals the characteristics of those men who recreate themselves in the very process of the struggle for socialism. Besides these two heroes of the Civil War era, Chapayev and Furmanov, both depicted with a gripping intensity, we see still other characters who round them out and make them stand out even more. Such characters include several commanders from Chapayev's division—simple and stern men deeply devoted to the revolutionary cause and full of decision, bravery, and vigor. One of the unforgettable figures is Chapayev's orderly, Petka, a lively young peasant—observant, gifted with a deep sensitivity, open to all the joys of youth—who dies gloriously as a hero of the revolution!

The Whites themselves are presented in an interesting and objective way. We see Chapayev's opponent, a colonel, whose experience of life and war has made him wise and who understands perfectly that his greatest danger is what lies behind him. That is why he would like to change the way the soldiers are treated by the officers. He does not want to be merely their stern commander, but also a "patriarchal" leader. But all his calculations are upset by the logic of the class struggle. The Whites' "psychological attack—which is, moreover, absolutely authentic—has a gripping effect. Here they are advancing in close columns, in an impeccable order and with affected daring, cigarettes dangling from their lips as they march to attack the positions held by Chapayev's division. Already some of the Red soldiers, seized by panic, are retreating. But Furmanov leads those fleeing back to the attack, and Chapayev, at the head of his cavalry, gives the enemy a decisive blow.

The film ends with Chapayev's disappearance, an episode that reproduces with great historical truth the glorious end of this legendary hero of the Civil War.

This "commentary," written in 1934, summarizes only some of the film's sequences, particularly the most spectacular ones. Let us compare it to our *découpage*, which passes briefly over those sequences already discussed in the above passage.

Sequence 1: Chapayev appears amidst the route of his soldiers and retrieves the situation.

Sequence 2: Chapayev the teacher, the rifle scene.

Sequence 3: Commissar Furmanov and the worker volunteers arrive.

Sequence 4: A noisy meeting between the worker volunteers and Chapayev's soldiers. Petka, Chapayev's orderly, demands silence: "Chapayev is thinking."

Sequence 5: In front of the map, Chapayev puts Furmanov to the test: "What does the commissar think about it?" Furmanov answers that they must follow the leader's decision, not that of someone who disagreed with Chapayev.

Sequence 6: The wounded man's tactical lesson, called the potato scene.

Sequence 7: Petka teaches Anna, the female worker volunteer, how to use a machine gun. He vainly tries to caress and seduce her.

Sequence 8: With the Whites. Colonel Borozdin explains to another, more traditional officer that one must treat subordinates in a more humane way and maintain a "patriarchal" relationship with them.

Sequence 9: First conflict between Chapayev and Furmanov. A veterinarian has complained to Furmanov that Chapayev demands that he arrogate for himself that title of doctor, a title he feels his abilities do not merit. Furmanov thinks the veterinarian is correct. "You defend this corrupt intelligentsia," says Chapayev; "you don't want a muzhik to be able to become a doctor." "He can't, he doesn't have the right," explains Furmanov.

Sequence 10: Furmanov educates Chapayev, teaching him the history of the past and of great leaders.

Sequence 11: With the Whites. The colonel's servant begs clemency for his brother who is about to be shot for desertion. The colonel grants it. Potapov's brother will be beaten instead.

Sequence 12: Second conflict between Chapayev and Furmanov. Increasingly, Chapayev's men have been stealing from the peasants. Furmanov has their lieutenant arrested. Chapayev is angry. "You bureaucrats, do you want to usurp another's glory? Who commands this division?" asks Chapayev. "You *and I,*" answers Furmanov. Chapayev's men and those of Furmanov almost come to blows. Furmanov has them return the stolen goods to the peasants, who come as a delegation to thank Chapayev. They say, "We could no longer distinguish the Whites from the Reds." Furmanov's modest victory.

Sequence 13: Petka expresses his admiration for Furmanov to Chapayev. "They wouldn't have sent a bad commissar to Chapayev," answers Chapayev.

Sequence 14: A meeting: Chapayev describes his conception of justice and of command to the peasants and soldiers.

Sequence 15: The last lesson. Anna knows how to load and unload the machine gun. Petka leaves on a reconnaissance mission; he is to bring back a prisoner. In the adieu scene, he doesn't dare kiss her. She is touched and for a long while watches him as he goes away.

Sequence 16: Petka takes prisoner the colonel's servant, who was fishing for food for his brother who was beaten and now lies dying. Touched, Petka lets him escape, keeping his rifle.

Sequence 17: At Chapayev's headquarters, Petka is reprimanded for not having brought back the prisoner.

Sequence 18: With the Whites. The colonel is playing the piano while his servant polishes the parquet floor. A close-up of Potapov's face reveals his anger, hatred, and a desire to murder the colonel. He does not have the strength to do it and explains to the colonel that his brother died of his wounds. The colonel expresses his grief.

Sequence 19: Red sentries are discussing Chapayev's good points. Furmanov goes by, checking their alertness and joking with them. A white soldier crosses the lines, going over to the Reds. It is Potapov.

Sequence 20: Potapov explains to Chapayev and Furmanov that the White offensive will take place the next day. "They are preparing a psychological attack."

Sequence 21: The eve of the battle. In the barracks Chapayev and Petka chat and sing "The Black Crow."

Sequence 22: The morning of the battle. Potapov is with the Reds. "Why are these men going to die?" asks a child. "In order to live," answers Potapov.

Sequence 23: Before the battle, Chapayev must leave the battlefield to suppress a mutiny. "We want to go home," say the soldiers. He executes one of the mutineers. Order is restored.

Sequence 24: The Whites' "psychological" attack involves music and the soldiers wear white gloves and march in step. Anna lets them come close in order to decimate them with the machine gun. Chapayev's cavalry pursues the Cossacks.

Sequence 25: After the victory. At the Whites' Headquarters, which the Reds now occupy, Chapayev congratulates Anna.

Sequence 26: Called to other duties, Furmanov departs and is replaced by another commissar, Sedov. Touching adieu with Chapayev.

Sequence 27: Chapayev's stanitsa is attacked at night by the Whites. Taken by surprise, the Reds must flee. Chapayev is wounded.

Sequence 28: The Whites pursue Chapayev who, with Petka's help, tries to reach the Orel River. In the fighting along the cliffs overlooking the river Potapov kills his former general.

Sequence 29: Chapayev wants to cross the Orel by swimming. A bullet hits him and he dies.

Sequence 30: The Red Cavalry arrives, ensuring a victory for the revolutionaries.

The lesson of this conclusion and the lessons of the entire film are clear. Heroes die but not the Communist party, which ensures a lasting victory. This lesson accompanies still another lesson in the film: that compared to heroes with good intentions, the men of the party show a calm and thoughtful superiority, and that, above all, the cause they are defending against the Whites is a just one. Contrasted with other testimonies of History, especially compared to Furmanov's text, which is at the base of the film, these lessons, notably the principal theme, reflect a certain premeditation.

The superiority of organization to spontaneity and anarchy is a theme that constantly crops up. Even if the term anarchy is never pronounced it is nontheless present, at least for a viewer in 1934, a viewer who knows about Russia's immediate past. In the sequence of the meeting (sequence 14), when a peasant asks Chapayev if he is for "the Bolsheviks or the Communists," Chapayev does not know what to answer. When the muzhik insists, Chapayev watches an amused Furmanov who smokes his pipe while awaiting Chapayev's answer with curiosity. After some hesitation, the latter answers that he is "for Lenin." The tense group then relaxes. Although a party member in 1934 knew quite well that the party changed its name in 1917, that the Social Democrat party (Bolshevik) became the Communist party, a certain ambiguity still remained for someone who also remembered that the term "Communist" was coupled with that of anarchist. In the film Chapayev obviously reveals his ignorance concerning the nuances of political vocabulary. Nonetheless, the effect of the sequence is still to dissassociate Chapayev from possibly belonging to any current other than the Leninist one, which, from that time on, was the only one identified with the revolution. Soon afterward another filmmaker, Yefim Dzigan, also removed the anarchists' role in We Are from Kronstadt [My iz kronstadt, 1936] by emphasizing only the politically anonymous agitation of those revolutionaries.

But the erasures of the Vasilievs do not stop there. They make Trotsky disappear: he is never referred to as the head of the Red Army even though the film's action takes place exactly at the time when he *was* at its head. His successor, Frunze, who commanded only one front at the time is named instead of him as the only one responsible for decisions coming from above. He is quoted several times, more than he deserves, as if to retroactively erase any memory of Trotsky from the viewer's mind.

Another *Chapayev* reference to Lenin, which can be understood only by old militants, is in sequence 18, when the colonel is playing what turns out to be the *Moonlight Sonata*. They would all have known that it was Lenin's favorite piece and that he had said that it was terrible to think that, while you were listening to the greatest works of beauty, dreadful dramas were taking place elsewhere. In the film, at exactly the moment when the colonel is playing the sonata, his servant's brother is dying.

However, the film does touch upon a problem that was essential in 1919 and that is dealt with in Furmanov's text: the nature of relations between old army officers who have been won over to the new regime and new commanders coming from the party ranks. In *Chapayev* only one allusion is made to this when, in the sequence of the test (sequence 5), the officer who expresses his disagreement concerning the envisioned tactic turns out to be an old army officer, as we can see by his uniform. This shot is framed in profile so that it is hardly visible. Thus, the problem is dodged here. In his book, however, Furmanov explains that from the moment he came to Chapayev to the moment he left, Chapayev was increasingly hostile to any collaboration with these officers. He also notes that this problem was disturbing. The reason for this erasure in the film is that any explicit allusion to this problem would have involved one of the quarrels between Trotsky and Stalin. In the final analysis, Stalin adopted his rival's position and used a significant number of officers of the old regime.

This explicit historical postulation is not innocent because it is systematic and one-sided. It even reaches out to the present time (that is, to the era when the film was made). It is characteristic that Furmanov and Chapayev are brought together concerning the peasant question at exactly the moment when collectivization necessitated bringing together the party and the peasant masses. Thus, the film's desired aim was, on the one hand, to legitimize the party's leadership and, on the other, to legitimize the dictatorship of the proletariat. It achieved these objectives since, as we have said, the authorities applauded the film and held it up as an example.

At this point it might be useful to proceed to another kind of analysis of the film in order to verify what messages it diffuses and what scenes were also seen as representing the views of the regime, even if the film's nonvisible content escaped directly from the will of its makers or the analysis of its contemporaries.

Diagram of the Film's Nonvisible Construction

An examination of the film's construction brings to light the opposition between two types of sequences: those that stage scenes of groups and masses where long shots dominate and those that stage scenes between two principal characters where close-ups are more numerous. The former, with a lyrical momentum, are basically animated by the collective movement of actors; the latter, which are more analytical, can be grouped in several ensembles as the diagram opposite shows. The numbers indicate the sequences in which the characters are found.

Thus, aside from sequences 16, 20, and 25, the most frequent combinations involve scenes between four couples: Chapayev and Furmanov: six sequences: 3, 5, 9, 10, 12, 26. Anna and Petka: three long sequences: 7, 15, 25. Petka and Chapayev: four sequences (often short): 3, 17, 21, 28. Borozdin and Potapov: four sequences (often short): 8, 11, 18, 28. Although these couples may also appear in other sequences, they do not play a central role in them. In sequence 25 Furmanov is present, but rather than intervening directly in the scene, he merely witnesses it. These couples play a central role in four narratives that can be isolated and thereby analyzed as narratives in themselves, independent of the film's thread and principal theme.

Using this diagram let us examine the evolution of the relationship between Chapayev and Furmanov, the principal "couple." From the beginning of the film they have relations of animosity, whereas in his text Furmanov explains that he had felt "enlightened" by the idea of seeing the famous Chapayev. Furmanov is reserved and polite in the film, following the line demanded by the ideology of the main narrative. Chapayev is aggressive; he hardly turns around when Furmanov introduces himself to him. Thus begins a genuine deal, a struggle for power.

Chapayev

	Chapayev	Formanov	Petka	Anna	Borozdin	Potapov
Chapayev		3,5,9,10, 12,26	13,17, 21,28	25		20
Formanov	3,5,9,10, 12,26					
Petka	13,17,21, 28			7,15, 25		16
Anna	25		7,15, 25			
Borozdin						8,11,18, 28
Potapov	20		16		8,11,18, 28	

At first this struggle follows certain rules and obeys traditions that are broken only when Chapayev bursts into Furmanov's room concerning the veterinarian incident, and then, to an even greater degree, when his lieutenant is arrested. At that time he threatens to come to blows and simulates the performance of a gladiator stripping off his medals. Then comes a sharp turning point in the relationship between the two men when the peasant delegation comes to thank Chapayev. After that this relationship keeps getting better until the two become brothers-in-arms. So rivalry becomes fraternity.

Relations between Anna and Petka also evolve from a negative to a positive pole. At the beginning, when the young female worker meets the soldier, a meeting symbolic of relations between city and country, Petka wants to have sexual relations with Anna. But Anna represents conscious revolution. She must prove herself virtuous and she refuses this type of relationship with Petka. She rejects him. Petka interests her because he teaches her how to handle a machine gun; although she is grateful to him for sharing his knowledge, duty calls. Nonetheless, she clearly has a fondness for him. The long embrace she bestows upon the barrel of the machine gun (sequence 15) is obviously meant for Petka. It hardly matters whether these sequences were the idea of the actress or the director, or if their meaning is conscious or unconscious. Besides, when Petka leaves on a mission that places his life in danger (thereby performing a ritual test in some way) she would like to embrace him before he leaves but does not dare. She controls herself in his presence, but as soon as he goes away she runs to the window to follow him with her eyes. The music underlines the nature of her feelings. After the victory (sequence 25), Petka and Anna have both accomplished their rite of passage. Petka has not merely taken a prisoner but has won him over, and Anna has dispersed the enemy with the machine gun. When Anna enters the warriors' barracks for the first time in order to receive Chapayev's congratulations, her liaison with Petka is henceforth legitimate and she lets him hold her around the waist. Chapayev, who is present, plays the role of the father and legitimizes their union in some sense by looking at Petka before speaking to Anna. The first thing Petka does after this act of recognition is to open an egg that Anna then swallows for her meal. The symbolic significance is unambiguous. Thus, this series of sequences goes from a condemnation of an illegitimate liaison to a justification of marriage.

The two other series of sequences present father-son relations between Chapayev and Petka and between the colonel and his servant. In the first case these relations function well. The father dies before the eyes of his son, who had taken on the role of father-protector when his wounded father needed youth's vigor. Conversely, relations between Borozdin and Potapov do not function well, although they were explicitly defined as "patriarchal." In a society condemned by History, fathers cannot exercise their protective function. In spite of his efforts the colonel does not succeed in saving the life of Potapov's brother. Thus, Potapov goes over to the enemy and kills the father who did not protect him.

Therefore, individual relationships are implicitly placed and evolve within the framework of the way a family functions, rather than within that of the class struggle. *Class struggle is only present in the general framework* of the war against the Whites. Was this because of the situation in 1934, when class relations in the countryside were never evoked? But in 1919 they were very much present. In this film "positive" and "normal" family relations function only within the society legitimized by History—that of the Soviets. Correlatively, the Vasilievs, who were in favor with the regime, judge the nature of a social system and of good and evil by the traditional functioning of the patriarchal family that constitutes the principle and the criterion of a regime's legitimacy.

Although this observation may appear paradoxical, it illustrates, at least *à minima*, the failure of Aleksandra Kollanti's ideas. But, in fact, its significance is given more weight in the film where it is corroborated by other elements that complete the model of values characterizing the regime of the Stalinist era. And this model constitutes at least a partial reversal of the value system of 1917 revolutionary society. This is also true, for example, of the attitude taken toward the institution of knowledge and that of military discipline.

The first conflict between the State (Furmanov) and society (Chapayev) breaks out over the problem of the legitimacy of degrees or titles. Chapayev believes that the success of the revolution means that everyone can have access to knowledge, with all that this implies, including the attainment of titles. For a man of the people such as Chapayev, the veterinarian and the doctor belong to the same world, that of knowledge. In this world roles and abilities can be interchanged. It is this interchangeability that allows Lenin and Trotsky (or Stalin) to rule on problems of science, art, and linguistics. But Furmanov sets him straight. Everyone does not have this right, and so a veterinarian cannot attain the rank of doctor: "He doesn't have the right." This reveals the ambiguity of the legitimacy at the base of the bureaucracy's power. While this legitimacy allows the bureaucrat Furmanov to act as divisional co-commander because he is a party member, it does not allow the veterinarian to act as a doctor. While the revolution has developed functional and social mobility *insofar* as one adheres to the party, in other cases such mobility is blocked. New divisions in society are thus established. *The new power reinstalls itself in the old knowledge*, whose forms are thereby revived. Furmanov has nothing to say about a piece of grafitti that makes Chapayev laugh except that "the versification is bad" (sequence 25).[2]

The retreat from revolutionary ideas is intensified in the

sequence concerning the military. In the Vasilievs' film Furmanov invites Chapayev "to dress with care" so that he can be recognized as a leader who "commands a division of the Soviet Army." And, in fact, Chapayev must change his outfit later on since the peasants do not recognize him (sequence 12). A bit further on we come to a comic sequence when Chapayev, in turn, counsels Petka to dress with care. Furmanov's narrative does not mention this concern for appearance. On the contrary, he writes that "one would have had to have been very clever to recognize the leaders." In addition, during the meeting sequence, Chapayev explains his ideas on discipline saying that the leader should be shot like anyone else if he disobeys the rules and that everyone is welcome at his table. But these articulated statements are contradicted by the film's images: we see the leaders and their men eating at separate tables. The commander's attitude during the mutiny scene (sequence 12) appears even more significant. The men who do not want to fight repeat exactly what the Russian soldiers said in 1917 when, encouraged by Lenin, they fraternized with the Germans. Here erasures help to totally change the meaning, for in the Vasilievs' film the mutineers are executed with the viewer's approval. Chapayev adds a sentence—not found in Furmanov's narrative—that springs from the heart of traditional morality: "The blood of the country's best sons will redeem your faults."

Let us add that the way the city assumed responsibility for rural areas is shown by a remarkable reversal. At the beginning of the film the batallion of worker volunteers is insignificant while Chapayev's division is all-important. Among these workers Anna symbolizes the city dweller's lack of skill. She learns to use a weapon while the leader Chapayev teaches tactics and strategy. At the end of the film, when Chapayev's staff is taken by surprise by the Whites in the early morning, the panic is widespread and Chapayev himself is at a loss. In a complete reversal of functions and roles, it is Anna the worker, who was unimportant at the beginning of the film and who also represents the party, who henceforth gives orders. From now on the countryside must simply obey the orders of the city that represents the central power.

Thus, the film implicitly identifies itself rather coherently with the Whites' system of values since it stresses redemption by blood, the myth of sacrifice, military discipline, the display of rank, the legitimacy of institutionalized knowledge, the glorification of the patriarchal and legitimate family, and submission to centralized power. We should also note that its attacks against a "corrupt intelligentsia" and the way it assimilates the officers into the intelligentsia (sequence 24) express another social tendency— the plebianization of ruling institutions—which was *one* of the characteristics of the Stalinist era.[3]

(1973–74)

NOTES

1. [Translator's note: According to Leyda (*Kino*, p. 314), the source of *Chapayev* "was one of the most modest and lasting literary works to come from the Civil War: Dmitiri Furmanov's *Chapayev*, an account of this individualist Red Army commander by the man sent to him as political commissar. In 1924 Furmanov had prepared a film treatment and submitted it, shortly before his death, to the Leningrad studio, where it was lost and forgotten. Early in 1932, Furmanov's widow submitted her own treatment to the same studio, where it was turned over to the Vasilievs. They found it good material and asked her permission to return to her husband's book as a base. Anna Furmanov agreed and turned over to them all her notes on the Chapayev days."]

2. The reinvestiture of traditional values is clear at all levels of the film, for example, in the music. Symphonic music, resonant with the themes of separation, victory, legitimate love, and death marks several sequences of the film.

3. On the origins and specific character of the Stalinist era, see my *The Russian Revolution of February 1917*, trans. J. L. Richards (Englewood Cliffs, N. J.: Prentice-Hall, 1972).

CHAPTER 4

Legend and History

Battleship Potemkin

In the case of the *Potemkin* mutiny, legend has managed to assume the appearance of truth. At certain moments the details of the narrative are authentic—from the worms crawling over the meat destined for the crew up to the great mutiny; and then, the solidarity of Odessa's inhabitants in favor of the victim, the repression and the massacre (which did not take place, however, on the Richilieu stairway), the departure of Constanta, and finally the way the ship broke through the blockade of "loyalist" ships which hailed the *Potemkin* with a salvo of "hurrahs" at the last moment. The spirit as well as some details of the legend are also authentic. Launched as a revolt by men who had been humiliated, the mutiny clearly marked the passage from individual paralysis to collective exaltation by means of an awakening of revolutionary consciousness which was unusual in the history of that era. But, as Wenden has succeeded in proving, the majority of the facts came from Einsenstein's imagination.[1]

However, in the midst of such a beautiful harmony, one

testimony—that of Einsenstein himself—is jarring. "In 1925," he writes, "this episode had been forgotten. . . . Whenever we spoke about the North Sea mutiny . . . we were immediately told about Lieutenant Schmidt and the *Ochakov*. The *Potemkin* mutiny had been still further erased from memory. It was hardly remembered and it was discussed even less." This failure of collective memory raises a problem which demands that we reconsider some aspects of the history of this mutiny and compare them with the legend.

The mutiny—which occurred on the ship considered the most "loyalist" of the North Sea fleet—was never really a part of the actions of the Social Democrat party (which, at Odessa itself, was evolving a very broad insurrectional movement that on the very eve of the mutiny was already at the stage of a successful general strike). Of course, there were revolutionary militants aboard the *Potemkin* and, in fact, they led the movement. However, neither their efforts, nor the additional ones of the delegates from the Social Democrat party of the Odessa section (who had boarded the ship) could succeed in turning the crew away from its tactical objectives—which were to rally the fleet to its cause. Thus, except for very curtailed operations, there was no coordinated action between the revolutionary movement in the city and the movement by the sailors; still less did the revolutionary organization of the party control their actions.

Furthermore, like the soldiers later on in 1917, the sailors of the *Potemkin*—most of whom had peasant origins—certainly fought for the defense of revolutionary values. But these were not necessarily the same values as those of the organizations. Proud of "their" ship, careful to see that order reigned on board (at least at the beginning), they performed maneuvers and loading with precision, as if on review. These sailors, like the soldiers in 1917, wanted to show that they didn't need disciplinary rules to accomplish their duty or to die.

Neither legend nor tradition really suggests the pitiful end of the invincible *Potemkin*. A part of the crew was put to flight by a handful of soldiers (at Fedosiya) while the rest surrendered a second time at Constanta. The ship ran aground. The sailors were exiled or sent to penal work camps; most of them emigrated to Argentina. None of them, it seems, rejoined the clandestine organizations of the "party of the revolution" or even played a role, however symbolic, in them. Legend and official documents removed this epilogue. One can imagine why, under these circumstances, legend and official history could retain only the initial phase of the *Potemkin* incident. And if Eisenstein's masterpiece had not revived it, even this cut version would perhaps have disappeared from people's memories since it is quite true that, in History, history often preserves only what legitimizes the power of those who govern.

The important point here is that official history, in Moscow, had to reintegrate the *Potemkin* into historical memory. At the edge of the Black Sea, because of "those who knew" in Georgia, official history was once more obliged to make the *Potemkin* disappear but for a different reason than before 1925—if it had evoked the victory of the *Potemkin* then all of official history, not only that of 1905, would have become suspect. And suspect, too, the legitimacy of those who base themselves on "the truth of history" to justify their right to govern.

(1976)

Gance's *Napoléon:* Like a Cathedral . . .

At the beginning of this century, who would have thought that, along with architecture, cinema would be the great Art of the future? A prophet might have imagined the masses of Europe and Asia for whom one had to build new cities, municipal buildings, and individual dwellings suited to the needs of societies emancipated by progress. . . . He might also have envisioned the public, the consumers of culture in a culture that would include cinema, this new popular art. He could not have imagined, however, the extent of his prophetic dreams; it would not have been possible to imagine that today, like a cathedral which invites additions from each new generation (or like the Louvre which is renewed before our eyes by an audacious pyramid built in its courtyard), Abel Gance's film *Napoléon* (1926) similarly adapts itself, thanks to music, to the needs of each generation.

Three elements cohabit this gigantic production:

1) sentences and words which, either through the titles or in other ways, convey the reality of the French Revolution;

70

2) images which reconstruct the Revolution in accordance with the vision of the filmmaker, who transposes and transfigures engravings of that era;

3) a musical score which was changed (even more than the editing) and which, in 1932, 1955, 1981, and 1984, served as a *method of regeneration* and brought the work up to date.

In the course of a half-century, a great deal has been said about the words and phrases Gance uses, about his proposed interpretation of the Revolution and of Bonaparte. As early as 1927, Léon Moussinac suggested that the film showed a Bonaparte for would-be fascists. True, the film expresses some of the ideas which constitute the kernal of fascist ideology: cult of the chief, scorn for and love of the crowd, and hostility toward political organizations and especially toward the Montagnards.[2] The last version of *Napoléon* (1980) is missing a significant exchange between Robespierre and Danton. At his trial Danton addresses the public and begins to say, "I think that . . ." when Robespierre taps him discreetly on the shoulder and whispers: "No, don't say 'I think that' but, rather, 'the people think that.' " There are other indications of this sort which are aimed at other political groups. One such instance is illustrated when Bonaparte does not want to fight in Vendée "against Frenchmen" but General Vendemiaire [another name for Napoleon] willingly opens fire upon a gathering of Royalists.[3] The cult of the chief, Bonaparte, who is identified with France and the Revolution, was held up as an ideal by an entire category of men who constituted a sort of political current during the 1920s. This current included old socialists who, transfigured by the war and seeing in the Soviet Revolution the repetition of the horrors of the Terror, called upon chiefs (without imagining that these new chiefs were to commit even more systematic crimes). In France Gustave Hervé, who was to make an appeal to Pétain in the 1930s, represented this current. The creation of the film *Napoléon*, film historian Jean Mitry tells us in his *Histoire du Cinéma*, was ordered by Westi, a German company run by Hugo Stinnes, one of the magnates who was to subsidize the Nazi party. As Mitry observes: "Doesn't Napoleon represent the dictator that Hugenberg and Stinnes wished for, a dictator capable of making order and justice reign for the benefit of capitalism?" Abel Gance enjoyed total freedom in making the film: he was asked only to exalt Bonaparte's energy, will, and magnetism. All these things, concludes Mitry, were quite sincerely part of the author's intentions.

Coincidences and lapses exist in other films by Gance: in *La fin du monde* (1930) the banker who outwits the author is called Schonburg, and the pawnbroker of *La dame aux Camelias* (1934) also has a Semitic profile. The reasons that made Abel Gance suspect in the eyes of left-wing critics become even clearer when we realize that he made a real "appeal to the chief" in his 1935 *Jérôme Perreau, héro des barricades*. It is true that Abel Gance was fascinated by all sorts of great men: he wanted, for example, to do an epic about Christopher Columbus. He might just as well have wanted to do one about Galileo, or Jesus, or Marx. But, as it happens, he dedicated *La vénus aveugle* to Pétain (the film's dedication was written in August of 1940). After Pétain's failure, the stunned seer was quiet until his marvelous *Paradis Perdu* (1940).

Did this giant of spectacle have any vision of history? Everything has been said about the creative genius of this visionary; no one has been able to top his exploits or equal his flashes of brilliance. Manipulating a double allegorical theme, he goes from Bonaparte, in a frail skiff, confronting an angry sea (whose turmoil mirrors that of the National Assembly) to the stormy Convention itself, which appears to sink as if in the tempest, reeling as if prey to the waves. This allegory of the tumult of the Terror is also embodied in a shaky ladder, about to fall, that is being climbed by the bureaucrat in charge of the dossiers of the victims of revolutionary tyranny.

The brilliance of Gance's practical inventions and techniques is also well known: in Corsica, to film Bonaparte fleeing before the police of Paoli, he placed a camera on the back of a galloping horse. Thus he could film what Bonaparte saw as he looked over his shoulder: the ascent and descent of the pursuing police riding over the hills.

This is what is essential in Abel Gance. For if the style of his images is often very close to Eisenstein's (notably the allegories and bestiary which govern the choice of faces), these two directors do not by any means organize their images according to the same theory of the whole. Here, *the story is the central narrative form*: it is constructed in accordance with the demands of *one* national memory—in this case, the anti-Robespierre tradition—that, in light of his own ideas, Gance chose to privilege. Eisenstein, on the other hand, *reconstructs* everything as he searches for the relationships between the visible and the non-visible; unlike Gance, he does not attempt to retrace an explicit event. Whereas Eisenstein *asks questions about history* and its modes of representation, Abel Gance is above all a man of *spectacle*. His maître à penser is neither Marx, nor Sorel, nor Auguste Comte; as Jean Tulard points out correctly, his ideal is Edmond Rostand.[4] Unbearable in the eyes of the avant-garde, this gradiose academicism has always pleased institutions, because it comforts and reassures them.

Still, the effect of the multiple versions he shot of *Napoléon* has been to narrow Gance's historical vision: at the beginning, in scenes that were eliminated, Tristan and his daughter Violine, simple and humble witnesses of Bonaparte's life, were to have linked (like the child in *The Bicycle Thief*) the spectator and the hero, balancing history seen from above—Great History—with a counterweight, i.e., History seen from below.

Where does truth lie in all this history? As with Eisenstein, myth triumphs over what really happened because there were never any snowball fights in Brienne, just as there was never any shooting on the Odessa steps. And Bonaparte's adieux to the Convention were dreamed up by Abel Gance, just as Einsenstein imagined most of the scenes in *Battleship Potemkin* and *October*.

With distance, one version of history replaces another but the work of art remains. And so, with the passage of time, our memory winds up by not distinguishing between, on the one hand, the imaginative memory of Eisenstein or Gance, and, on the other, history such as it really happened, even though historians seek to make us understand and artists seek to make us participate. And insofar as we participate in the survival of the film, it matters little to Gance that different musical scores were added to his film. So much the better if the scores regenerated it, adapting it to the successive needs of later spectators. It is hard to deny that the last musical adaptation wants to please: a kitschy potpourri of all the motifs and themes in the repertory from Offenbach to "ça ira,"[5] from Strauss to Wiener, it operates with the spirit of Carnival . . . to make us happy.[6]

(1987)

Film: Source of History

NOTES

1. D. J. Wenden, "Battleship Potemkin," in K. R. M. Short, ed., Feature Films as History, (University of Tennessee Press, 1981).
2. [Translator's Note: The Montagnards were radical members of the National Assembly after the French Revolution. The best-known leaders, all opposed to the more moderate Girondins, were Danton, Marat, and Robespierre.]
3. [Translator's Note: The "Wars of Vendée" designates a series of counterrevolutionary insurrections, begun in 1793, of peasants of the Vendée region who were incited by the propaganda of nobles and clergy opposed to the Revolution. The outbursts had still not been extinguished when Napoleon crushed an uprising in 1815.]
4. [Translator's Note: Edmond Rostand was a nineteenth-century French playwright best known for Cyrano de Bergerac.]
5. [Translator's Note: "Ça ira" was a song of the Revolution, of the "sans-culottes."]
6. For more on Abel Gance, see Roger Icart, Abel Gance; ou, Le Prométhée foudroyé (Lausanne: L'age d'homme, 1983).

CHAPTER 5

Film and the Legitimization of Power in the Soviet Regime

More than in any country, and earlier than anywhere else, the problem of the use and role of imagery has been studied in the Soviet Union and especially by those in the government and by those holding other forms of power. Since the October Revolution, there has been a clear relationship between, on the one hand, the attitude of the Communist party toward films and, on the other hand, the production of films and television programs. But the meaning of this relationship has changed at least twice.

During a first period (roughly from 1917 to the end of the 1920s) I would say that a misunderstanding about legitimization existed between filmmakers and those in political power. During a second period, which began at the end of the twenties, this misunderstanding ended and a standardized legitimization came into effect. In the course of the last fifteen years one can see that this standardized legitimization has given way, and today it would be more precise to speak of a thwarted legitimization because of the existence of a gap between film and television production.

Naturally, I am speaking of overlapping periods rather than strictly delimited ones.

First Period: Misunderstanding over Legitimization

Discussing films and the problem of cinema in the Soviet Union in 1923, Trotsky wrote: "We Bolsheviks, we are stupid not to have captured cinema, not to have controlled filmmaking." Trotsky meant that movies had to become a tool to counterbalance church and obscurantism, and that cinema had to take the place of the tavern. In the early 1920s it is obvious that for him, and in a certain way for Lunacharsky also, films should be used, at least in the short run, for educational purposes more than as tools of propaganda. He did not consider film an art form, but rather an educational instrument of acculturation.

Why? Because for the Bolsheviks, that is, for people who came from the elite of the bourgeoisie or even from the aristocracy and the upper classes (Lenin, Kollontaï, etc.), movies were entertainment for the people, for the masses. They themselves were not interested in films; readers of books and newspapers, they seldom visited film theaters. That explains why, when they wanted to control the production of films, they were interested only in the textual aspect of films, or in their themes, scenarios, or scripts. In the beginning they assumed that comedies, dramas, and other such genres had no political meaning. They paid attention to newsreels and documentary films rather than to fictional films.

The Bolshevik leaders ignored the gap that existed between script and images; they were not at all interested in filmmaking itself and had no opinions about these kinds of problems. On the contrary, for an artist, the specificity of filmmaking is not in the script but in action, in montage. But Eisenstein and for Dziga Vertov, montage was a way to reconstruct or rebuild reality, not merely a way to reproduce reality.

The result of this misunderstanding was rather strange: since those in power were always speaking about workers, soldiers, and peasants, and not about themselves, the filmmakers made newsreels and fictional films about soldiers, workers, and peasants, forgetting the leaders, the Bolsheviks. In a certain way, this explains why in *Strike*, or in *Mother*, we can see many activists, but the Bolsheviks are absent—completely absent. Hiding their weapons, the workers are supposed to be anarchists or Socialist Revolutionaries, not social democrats. The Bolsheviks are only honored by short quotations from Lenin at the beginning or the end of each reel. The actual origin of this misunderstanding rests on the fact that for citizens and for artists, the legitimization of the 1917 Revolution was based not on the specific actions of the Bolsheviks but on the action of the masses on History.[1]

In *Dura Lex*, a film made by Kuleshov in 1926, one can observe an attack against popular justice and even the Soviet system. In a certain way this masterpiece is an unconscious witness to History. That is why the newspapers and the political leaders did not like, at least in the beginning, the great films made by Pudovkin, Kuleshov, and even Eisenstein. It was only after their success in western Europe, especially after the success of *Battleship Potemkin* in Berlin, "Capital of the World Revolution," that the Communist leaders changed their minds and began to announce that the Soviet Union had become the country of the renewal of the seventh Art. Indeed, they became very proud of this fact. At the same time they came to understand Trotsky's remark that they needed to keep an eye on the process of film production in their country. From then on, filmmaking came under surveillance.

Second Period: Standardized Legitimization

Nonetheless, the government continued to disapprove of the great filmmakers because they were in a certain way much too independent in their vision of society, in spite of their endeavors to satisfy the new regime. This disapproval of the great filmmakers can also be explained by a second reason: Eisenstein, Dziga Vertov, and others did their utmost to conform to the government's wishes, but people were now avoiding their films because these artists were too avant-gardist and hard to be appreciated and understood by common people. This was the case, for instance, with *October* and *Man with a Camera* [*Chelovek S. Kinoapparatom*, Dziga Vertov, 1929]. Considering themselves the avant-gardists of a new art form, these filmmakers had the same attitude that characterized Picasso, for example, when his master-pieces were no longer understood by the public. This attitude was abetted by a specific evolution in the social structure of the Soviet political system. During this period (the end of the 1920s to the beginning of the 1930s), the phenomenon of the plebeianization of civil institutions and of political power had the effect of introducing—even at the top of the state apparatus—people who were not very educated and who disliked the abstractions of the great filmmakers.

On the other hand, the more traditional filmmakers, who were not supposed to be flag wavers for the Soviets but were only providing entertainment for the people (Ermler, Barnet, Room, etc.), were accused of making films that lacked political meaning and that were much too superficial. As a result of the conjuncture of these two trends, cinematographic activity as a whole came under reconsideration.

These reasons explain why films changed completely during the Zhdanovist period. Films were made to legitimize the Communist party and those bureaucrats and heroes who would play a new role in society. Eisenstein, Kuleshov, Pudovkin, and others were expelled from the field of production and replaced by a new generation of filmmakers—the most famous of whom were Dovzhenko, the Vasilievs, and Jutkevich. In their films, the heroes were the people who were glorified by the Stalinist state: the kolkhozniki, traktoristy, and even the apparatchiki. In my opinion, the first film that introduces a new style and a new category of heroes is Jutkevich's *Krujeva* [1928], in which young apparatchiki are seen as the expression of a new society because they create a new atmosphere in the club they are organizing. But, naturally, the main hero remains the Communist party, and, from this point of view, the principal masterpiece of this period is *Chapayev* by Sergei Vasiliev and Georgi Vasiliev. In this film, through the legitimization of the Commissar and the appearance of the legitimization of the Reds' struggle against the Whites, the new values of the system are also legitimized. These new values are also the traditional values of family (and not free love); obedience in the army (rather than the free election of the officers); and reflection and analysis (as opposed to spontaneity).

78

Although these are not openly propounded, they become evident through analysis of the film. (See Chapter 3.)

This period may thus be considered as one of standarized legitimization, both because many films were constructed under the same rules and, even more so, because there was *no gap between the reproduction of society* in newsreels and *the reconstruction of reality* in fictional films. The filmmakers produced the same kinds of shots in fiction as in documentary films (cf. Dovzhenko).

Third Period: Thwarted Legitimization

In the last fifteen years, the main legitimization has come not from cinema, but from television. As Kristian Feigelson wrote, television is now playing the role of the *Agitprop* of the 1930s. We can see programs which show us people who provide examples and models to imitate. The values of the regime are presented every day on Soviet television.[2] That is why it has become necessary for filmmakers to make films different from the television films. Otherwise, the movie theaters would be empty.

We can observe that the new directions taken by Soviet films are, to a certain extent, opposed to the conformist representation of society that can be seen on television. They include:

—Science fiction films (*Stalker* [1980] by Tarkovsky, for example), which are too expensive for television production.

—Films showing a new vision of society. The first ones were perhaps Tarkovsky's *Ivan's Childhood* [*Ivanovo detstro*] in 1962 and Klimov's *Welcome* [*Dobro pozalovat'*, 1964]. These films depict nonconformist visions of war and pioneer groups. In the last ten years many masterpieces, such as *Ja sprosu slovo* [Panfilov, 1976] have been produced in this genre.

—Films analyzing society through the lives of marginal people, who are, in a certain way, anti-heroes. Suskin is one of the filmmakers who has chosen this new kind of "hero."

—Films reconstructing the past without adopting a negative approach.

—Many films produced in the republics (Turkmenistan, etc.), which also represent a new vision, one completely disconnected from the Soviet spirit. An example of this kind of film is *Chaksem i Garib* [1963] by Tahib Sabirov. Films in this genre sometimes even come out of Iran and Iraq. They can also be Mongolian films, which may actually be produced in China or elsewhere. The films made in Georgia often seem to us very witty in their critical approach to the system.

The social and cultural movement of the last fifteen years should reinforce this evolution toward a more liberated filmmaking. The development of a highly educated populace is creating new needs that only this new kind of film can satisfy. We may call this progression in Soviet film evolution, but it is so diametrically opposed to the thinking of the late 1920s and 1930s that it could almost be called a revolution.[3]

In conclusion, one can say that it is harder to control films and images than texts because of the cultural gap existing between the state apparatus and society. But also, because there is a need to make money and to provide entertainment, films have to produce images completely different from those of the typographic characters of *Pravda* to attract an audience.

(1986)

NOTES

1. Marc Ferro, *The Bolshevik Revolution: A Social History of the Russian Revolution* (London: Routledge & Kegan Paul, 1985), pp. 142–44.
2. Kristian Feigelson, "En URSS, la télévision a-t-elle pris la relève de l'Agitprop?" in M. Ferro, ed., *Film et Histoire* (Paris: Études des hautes études en sciences sociales), 1984.
3. Marc Ferro, "Y a-t-il trop de démocratie en URSS?" *Annales* (ESC) 4, July–August, 1985.

CHAPTER 6

Analysis of Societies and Different Types of Films

All films are objects for analysis. Certainly, at the present time only newsreels and documentaries are considered documents. Fictional films—"cinema"—are seen in relation to the imaginary and not to knowledge; they are not seen as an expression of reality but as a representation of it. Today, because the dogmas and customs of written tradition have been transposed to images, little trust is placed in the *scientific* testimony of fiction which appears similar to novels. Everyone knows that serious people—men of science or politics, administrators, and men of decision—have little faith in the novel or the imagination. In the East, they would rather trust numbers and statistics, and in the West, computations of profit. Historians and economists are just like them in this respect. However, we know the consequences of this faith in science. For example, in principle, agricultural production in the East should have continued to grow while Western experts felt that the price of oil should have kept going down.

Thus, by likening the film in some sense to writing, educated people tend to accept, if pressed, the testimony of the documentary film but not the film as a document. For them the film works only with dreams, as if dreams were not part of reality, or as if the imagination were not one of the motives of human activity.

Coming back to the reciprocal role of documentaries (and newsreels) and of fictional films (the "cinema") in the analysis of societies, contrary to popular belief, fictional films offer (aside from any comparisons concerning their essence) a practical advantage over newsreels and documentaries. Thanks to the analysis of critical reactions, to the study of the number of viewers who see them and to what we know concerning the conditions of production, it is possible to approach at least some of the relations between film and society. And the same cannot always be said for newsreels or film documents.[1]

In other respects, even if the nature of the social reality presented by fictional films is not the same as that offered by documentaries or newsreels, there are nonetheless grey zones where these two types of film intermingle and where the distinction between them is less absolute than it might seem. It is clear that films shot outdoors furnish much documentry information which resembles that found in reportage, even if the *function* of such information is not the same in both types of films. This information—which we will call a "filmic museum of objects and gestures, of attitudes and social behavior"—often comes from the director involuntarily. As we have said, a film is always submerged by its content.

Thus certain films of Jean-Luc Godard—such as *Deux ou Trois Choses que je sais d'elle* [*Two or Three Things I Know About Her*, 1967]—are as much reportage as they are fiction. This is true of a good number of the films of the English school of the 1970s.

Each film has a value as a document, whatever its seeming nature. This is true even if it has been shot in the studio, and even if it neither narrates nor depicts. By the way it affects people's imaginary universe, and by the very imaginary universe that it conveys, every film posits a relation between its author, its subject matter, and the viewer. Besides, if it is true that the not-said and the imaginary have as much historical value as History, then the cinema, and especially the fictional film, open

82

a royal way to psycho-socio-historical zones never reached by the analysis of "documents."

The bards of cinema are fully convinced of this. All the same, it seems that they, too, tend to create a hierarchy of "cinematographic" genres. For example, they deny that a television broadcast is as much a part of cinema as cinema itself. These distinctions stem from the customs and defense mechanisms of the profession. In France the alibi of censorship authorizes itself, often with paradoxical effects. Directories and catalogues do not list the historical programs that Frédéric Rossif made for television, even though the nature of such programs is the same as the films he made to be shown in theaters.

Certainly, genres exist in cinema as they do in written production. Documentaries, musical comedies, and montage films are distinct from each other, and each involves a different kind of cinematographic work. But for purposes of social and cultural analysis, they are all documentary objects. Besides, the cinematographic work of Elia Kazan, or even of Vincente Minnelli, tell and teach a great deal about America. One needs only to know how to read them. And film reportage is not necessarily more objective, more scientific, or more "real." Let me propose the following paradoxical hypothesis: the role of the imaginary and the ideological in the outlook of the Michelangelo Antonioni who filmed the documentary *China* [1972] was no less important than the role of social reality and analysis in *Il Grido* [*The Cry*, 1957] or *Il Deserto Rosso* [*Red Desert*, 1964], two works of imagination by this same Antonioni.

The paradox is only a seeming one. In a reversed manner, it reopens the old quarrel raised by great directors of the silent era. For Dziga Vertov only documentaries presented reality and documents came only from the outside world. The camera's eye possessed the "truth." On the other hand, Einsenstein felt that a deeper and more real analysis of social functioning could be reached through the language of montage, a precision instrument which permitted any and all reconstructions and gave priority to recreation and editing. (Such reconstruction, and not mere reconstitution, means that the filmmaker becomes a social scientist, a historian.) A third viewpoint was introduced by Jean Vigo who felt that what he offered—a documented viewpoint—was better than a document or an analysis. Joris Ivens belongs to this last school, while the naturalist films of Robert J. Flaherty, Georges Rouquier, and Alexander Dovzhenko—at the crossroads of all these currents—imply that observation involves participation given that truth, too, involves a desire for beauty. The school of Jean Rouch and Luc de Heusch cannot conceive of a document without a viewpoint. Unlike Jean Vigo, these filmmakers aim at analysis, and their works are presented as quasi-experimental and scientific research documents. This raises the issue of the ideology of "documentary," as well as anthropological, film.

Another paradox is that historical reconstructions may have hardly any historical reality. Let us take another look at masterpieces such as *Alexander Nevsky* or *Andrei Rubylov* which reproduce the past in an exemplary manner. It is no longer possible to understand and imagine medieval Russia without mentally banishing Eisenstein's or Tarkovsky's haunting images. In this sense *Alexander Nevsky* and *Andrei Rubylov* are two extraordinary object films. However, they are nothing more than that, a bit the way Jules Michelet's *Introduction à l'histoire universelle* (1831) is an object book. The past reconstructed by these films is a mediated past. Through the choice of themes, the tastes of the era, production necessities, the force of the writing, and the creator's omissions, we see the Soviet Union of 1970 as its opponents experienced it. Clearly, this is where the true historical reality of these films is found and not in the way they represent the past (aside from authentic costumes or fragments of dialogues.) In the same way, *Jud Süss* is more important for its vision of Hitlerian ideas and of what Nazism thought it had to tell the Germans about Jews, than for its depiction of eighteenth-century Germany.

Although it is easy to believe cinema incapable of depicting the past, how can we date the religious ceremony—where the ritual has remained unchanged since the sixteenth century—filmed by Pierre Gauge? Seen *backward*, the scene in *The General Line* [*Generalnaya Linya*, Eisenstein, 1929] where the house is taken apart, operation after operation, shows how isbas were built in ancient Russia. Such examples could be multiplied and, put together, they could constitute a sort of living museum of the past.

All this proves to what degree historians and sociologists do not establish the same categories as a film historian to distinguish among different cinematic genres. Nonetheless, the distinction between documentary films and fictional films remains operational insofar as these two types of films often draw upon cinematographic work which, despite some similarities, is essentially different because of the different nature of the original *rushes*. We will examine some of the modalities of construction and analysis presented by extreme forms of film, from the raw document, or one that is considered such, up to fictional and even science-fiction films. To be strictly logical I should have gone even further, from the automatic and continuous recording of everything that happens and is said everywhere simultaneously (an imaginary situation depicted in *THX-1138* [George Lucas, 1971]) to non-narrative, nonrepresentational films such as those studied by G. Fihman and C. Eyzickman. Such a project, however, would have gone beyond the bounds of this work.

(1975)

NOTES

1. Since the advent of television, and thanks to this medium, we can better compare the relationship of these two filmic "categories" to society. But we are badly informed about television. It seems that those in charge of it believe that the content of a documentary film risks having a direct effect upon viewers and, for this reason, these documentary films are very rarely the subject of discussion. However, we do not know if this "producers' fear" is well founded.

Ideological unorthodoxy: Rene Clair's A *nous la libertè*. (Photo courtesy of The Museum of Modern Art/Film Stills Archive.)

Kuleshov's *Dura Lex:* "Hidden behind Canada lies Russia." (Photo courtesy of The Museum of Modern Art/Film Stills Archive.)

Reconstructing the Soviet past: Eisenstein's *Alexander Nevsky*. (Photos courtesy of The Museum of Modern Art/Film Stills Archive.)

Another reconstruction of the Soviet past: *Andrei Rublov*. (Photos courtesy of The Museum of Modern Art/Film Stills Archive.)

Eisenstein's *Strike*: Attacked in their homes! (Photo courtesy of The Museum of Modern Art/Film Stills Archive.)

Strike: A wandering child provokes the strike. (Photo courtesy of The Museum of Modern Art/Film Stills Archive.)

The prisoners dream of escape in Pudovkin's *Mother*. (Photo courtesy of The Museum of Modern Art/Film Stills Archive.)

Mother: A mother's agony and her political awakening. (Photo courtesy of The Museum of Modern Art/Film Stills Archive.)

Tactical lessons in *Chapayev*: Heroes die but not the Communist party. (Photo courtesy of The Museum of Modern Art/Film Stills Archive.)

Unions in the House of Trade in Moscow during a public discussion devoted to *Chapayev*, November 30, 1934. In the background hang portraits of the principal heroes of the film: *right*, Chapayev; *left*, Furmanov. (Photo courtesy of The Museum of Modern Art/Film Stills Archive.)

Eisenstein's glorious *Potemkin!* (Photo courtesy of The Museum of Modern Art/Film Stills Archive.)

Battleship Potemkin: Vermin infested food. (Photo courtesy of The Museum of Modern Art/Film Stills Archive.)

Napoléon: Cult of the Chief.
(Photo courtesy of The Museum
of Modern Art/Film Stills Archive.)

Godard's *Two or Three Things that
I Know about Her:* "Just as much
reportage as fiction."

Choosing the enemy. The horrors of Germany and Japan: Chaplin's *The Great Dictator*, Frank Borzage's *The Mortal Storm* and Dmytryk's *Behind the Rising Sun* (photo courtesy of The Museum of Modern Art/Film Stills Archive.)

And the wonders of Russia: The honest Soviet leaders in *Mission to Moscow*; Soviet patriots under attack, and "a small-town paradise in the Ukraine" in *The North Star*.

Paths of Glory: The arbitrariness of military justice.

An innocent executed for *"King and Country."*

Orson Welles as Harry Lime in *The Third Man*: A moral of ambiguity. (Photo courtesy of The Museum of Modern Art/Film Stills Archive.)

Alida Valli as Anna in *The Third Man:* A modern Antigone. (Photo courtesy of
The Museum of Modern Art/Film Stills Archive.)

The ambiguities of Renoir's *La grande illusion:* The French Jew and the German woman (Marcel Dalio and Dita Parlo) (*above*); the aristocrat and the
working man (Pierre Fresnay and Jean Gabin) (*bottom of opposite page*).

Jud Süss: The dark face of anti-Semitism. (Photo courtesy of The Museum of Modern Art/Film Stills Archive.)

Le chagrin et la pitié: Do all interviews have equal weight? Louis Grave, former Resistance fighter, now an Yronde farmer.

M: The court of criminals embodies popular sentiment. (Photo courtesy of The Museum of Modern Art/Film Stills Archive.)

Salt of the Earth or Liberty and Justice for all: Workers, women, and Indians.
(Photo courtesy of The Museum of Modern Art/Film Stills Archive.)

FILM: AGENT OF HISTORY

CHAPTER 7

Concentration Camps in the Soviet Union: An Information Breach

A good number of experiments are needed if we are to learn how a film affects society. But are such experiments trustworthy? In an article devoted to investigating the effects of violence in cinema and television (in *Communications*, No. 7, 1966) André Glucksman seems to think they are not. It is true that the projection of *Jud Süss* in Marseilles in 1942 was followed by anti-Semitic demonstrations, but correlations of this sort are rather rare. Here another sort of correlation will be analyzed: the ways a French television broadcast of a film on concentration camps in the Soviet Union affected people in France, awakening reactions which are as significant as the documentary itself. The French Communist party did not go along with the Soviet thesis of the "great falsehood." It condemned the existence of work camps without questioning the authenticity of the evidence.

Thus, once more, a filmic document broke through a very closed system of traditional information. In the face of official information and culture which is controlled by the ruling class, the P.C.F. [French Communist party] founded its own counter-culture with an arsenal of theories, beliefs, and certitudes. Images have shaken this system.

But each day images could open other breaches in each information system if television were closer to the viewers and if its depiction of "French" society were less antiseptic, less enslaved to ensconced interests—if it were free.

Every work camp is a crime against humanity. Seeing this one where these Soviet prisoners are assembled, however, would certainly have led one to think that this "penal colony" near Riga is a thousand times less horrible than ones we have seen in Chile, in Germany, in Spain. If this document has not evoked comments to this effect, it is because, by dint of locking themselves into a conceptual and verbal code, by repeating that there are no political prisoners in the U.S.S.R., Soviet leaders have managed to reach an objective which is totally opposed to what they wanted: this document has been seen only as a proof that they were lying.

And French Communists have correctly understood that the visual era makes it impossible for institutions and opponents to lie. The important fact is that they have thereby recognized that information doesn't have to emanate from their needs to be true. They say it is willed by necessity—perhaps. The P.C.F. nonetheless implicitly recognizes that a monopoly makes information impossible. This is what constitutes the significance of what has occurred.

A structure protected by barbed wire, with a lookout man upon a sort of belvedere. Neither this observation post nor the protecting wall are particularly imposing, nor even high. It all seems rather ordinary. Green uniforms, red epaulettes, militia or soldiers mount guard accompanied by police dogs. Suddenly, prisoners appear, densely surrounded by militia. You can count about sixty of them, perhaps a hundred. They walk in rows, with normal steps, without giving the appearance of being under strict orders. But the presence of the dogs, which are frequently in the field of vision, bears witness to close and constant supervision.

We see the prisoners once again. Are they returning from a work yard? Then we see prison trucks transporting them. Drivers cross paths, joke; a truck stops and, it seems, also another one, as if the convoy were stopping; drivers and guards kid each other, one goes off to urinate, laughingly greets someone in the camera's field. A police dog reappears.

The film lasts around eight minutes. It is silent and in color. Some "blanks" in the middle of the document indicate a stoppage in the shooting. There is no apparent construction in this film, no editing or cuts or adjunction of extra-filmic documents such as titles or other inserts. Consequently, it is not a question of an elaborated film, which has been worked over, reconstructed, or cut, but rather of an uninterrupted document (except for the pauses) seized by the camera. The succession of scenes (which are sometimes "empty" and sometimes not) joined together offers a supplementary proof that the film has not been gone over and revised after being printed.

Consequently, it is a raw and authentic document, and one that has been shot in precarious conditions as we can see by the trembling which occurs before and after the zoom shots. Since the angle of shots varies little and the background of the setting returns several times, we can assume that the film was shot from one or two fixed points—either from a thicket or a bend in the road, or from the inside of a car which stopped and moved on—from a distance varying between ten to twenty-four meters from the places filmed. All this could imply that the cameraman was hiding but that he had relative freedom of access to the places filmed. The only indication to the contrary is that one of the guards makes a gesture to someone, but perhaps it was not meant for the camerman but rather for a colleague in the field of vision.

A raw documentary but neither accidental nor innocent, this film was made to bear witness. This is proved by two details. The zoom shots and close-ups deal solely with indications of locale—the plates of the trucks, place names in Latin or Cyrillic characters—which serve to authenticate the documentary. Another proof of the cameraman's intentions is that the longest shots deal with the prison regime—barbed wire, lookout posts, surrounding walls. The only other long shots depict living scenes such as the guards' break.

We can see that it is not a question of a "concentration universe," nor of a Nazi type camp nor even of a great "modern" prison like some that exist in France or the United States. The structure suggests rather a no-trespassing zone, one that might be near a military camp situated near the outskirts of a big city. If and when they venture there, the city's inhabitants would know perfectly well that prisoners were behind the walls, but the no-entry signs would limit access and visibility.

Besides concentration camps, other more ordinary modes of incarceration also exist. In all probability this one is not a concentration camp (*Lager*) but a penal "colony" containing those condemned to less than three years of forced labor. Those who are condemned to more than three years would be placed in more isolated camps, far from big cities. Let us note that the letters *Lag* which appear on one of the trucks do not mean anything special. On other vehicles one can read *Lat*, or *Las*.

The claim on the part of Soviet officials that the film represents a "great falsehood" comes from the fact that when it was shown the documentary was announced as a film on "concentration camps" for "political detainees." It is not exactly a question of a "camp" but of a "colony" whose penal regime is more flexible, with salaries and possible reductions in sentences for those who surpassed required "norms." As for the fact that it deals with ordinary criminals, there is no way of proving such an assertion since, officially, there are no political prisoners in the Soviet Union. Whoever is not satisfied with the regime is considered an enemy of society and consequently defined as an offender; or else he is considered abnormal and treated as such.

(1976)

CHAPTER 8

On American Anti-Nazism, 1939–43: Fragments

France—United States, 1939: Choosing the Enemy

"If you accuse me of being anti-Nazi, you would be right . . . and if you accuse me of producing films which emphasize the necessity of increasing national defense, you would be right again." God knows what French producer on the eve of World War II would have uttered these words Darryl F. Zanuck addressed to the subcommittee headed by D. Worth Clark and delegated by J. P. Kennedy, B. K. Wheeler, and G. T. Nye to investigate "warmongers." Moreover, Zanuck's lawyer Wendell Wilkie, the "pacifist" candidate against Roosevelt, added: "There's no need for an investigation since we all detest Nazis here."

Any list you might make of anti-German or anti-Nazi films shown in Paris in 1939 would not be very long. Aside from *Entente cordiale* (Marcel L'Herbier, 1938), *Double crime sur la ligne Maginot* (Félix Gandéra, 1937), and *Les disparus de Saint-Agil* (Christian-Jaque, 1938), which cast an anonymous doubt on the Germans' hidden motives, there is not a single film which is explicitly anti-Nazi, except *Confessions of a Nazi Spy* [Anatole Litvak, 1939], which is an American film.

Concerning *Double crime sur la ligne Maginot* and other French films, the critic for the *New York Times* wrote, "In view of Warner Brothers' current alarming expose of Nazi spy activities in America, it is surprising to discover that the French, who would seem to have more reason to be disturbed by this situation, are quite casual in the face of a menace which apparently faces all of us" (May 8, 1939). That same year in the United States eighteen explicitly anti-Nazi films were shown (such as *Beasts of Berlin* and *U-Boat 29*), to which we must add three anti-Nazi films among the sixteen Soviet films shown in New York: *The Oppenheims* [*Semya Oppenheim*, Grigorij Roshal, 1939], *Swamp Soldiers* [*Bolotnyie soldati*, Alexsandr Macheret, 1938], and *A Great Citizen* [*Veliki grazhdanin*, Fridich Markovitch Ermler, 1938–39]. In counterpoint, the Americans produced or showed two anti-Soviet films: *Ninotchka* [Ernst Lubitch, 1939] (also shown in Paris) and *Sky Patrol* [Howard Bretherton, 1939], which condemned Soviet intervention in Finland.

This balance sheet clearly shows that—unlike France, where the atmosphere was one of embryonic civil war and where military or cultural rules did not really try to define whether the enemy was Communism or Nazism—in the United States the choice was made in a definite way even before 1939. In 1938 films such as the following were projected—*The Last Train from Madrid* [James Hogan, 1937] and *Three Comrades* [Frank Borzage, 1938]. This choice was more marked in the world of film than in that of either journalism or investigative writing where—even in the landmark year of 1939—several pro-Nazi works such as E. Hambloch's *Germany Ramparts* (and others which justified German policies after 1944) appeared, while the majority of writings dealing with the U.S.S.R. were anti-Soviet (witness the works of P. A. Sloan, C. Clark, and Krivisky).

The attitude of American filmmakers and producers might be explained by the supposition that a majority of them were either refugee filmmakers from Germany or Jews of German and American origin. Certainly *some* of them were, and it is conceivable that they inspired anti-Nazi momentum, but most of them were not Jews or refugees. Moreover, when these same filmmakers took refuge from Germany in France they were not able to exert the same influence.

Once war was declared President Roosevelt gave precise instructions in the aim of developing a cinema that would glorify just law and American values. Although France was already in a state of war between September, 1939, and June, 1940, no anti-Nazi films were produced there. In the United States, however, the anti-Nazi movement continued to grow. It had taken off decisively from the beginning of the World War II (*Confessions of a Nazi Spy* even dates from April, 1939) with *Four Sons* [Archie Mayo, 1940], *Escape* [Mervyn LeRoy, 1940], *The Great Dictator* [Chaplin, 1940], *Foreign Correspondent* [Alfred Hitchcock, 1940], and especially Frank Borzage's *The Mortal Storm* [1939], which (by its appeal to Germans to overthrow Hitler) gave rise to a diplomatic incident.

A study of American ideology seen through the cinema of the war years should concentrate upon certain groups of films, in addition to documentaries and newsreels.

a) Very successful anti-Nazi films, such as *The Man I Married* [Irving Pichel, 1940] and *Confessions of a Nazi Spy*, as well as those which, despite good reviews, found no audience, such as Irving Pichel's "total commercial flop" *The Moon Is Down* [1943] and Jean Renoir's *This Land Is Mine* [1943].

b) Anti-Japanese films which were few in number but often successful such as Edward Dmytryk's *Behind the Rising Sun* [1943].

c) Great box-office hits. According to records in *Variety* (no. 269, 1972), those in the lead, after *Gone With the Wind* [Victor Fleming, 1939], which continued to dominate the pack two years after its release, were: Michael Curtiz's *This Is the Army* [1943] (based on Irving Berlin's musical); Sam Wood's *For Whom the Bell Tolls* [1943]; Howard Hawks's *Sergeant York*, William Wyler's *Mrs. Miniver*; John Cromwell's *Since You Went Away* [1944] (produced by David O. Selznick); Michael Curtiz's *Yankee Doodle Dandy* [1942]; Mervyn LeRoy's *Thirty Seconds Over Tokyo* [1944]; Victor Fleming's *A Guy Named Joe* [1943]; and Edmund Goulding's *Claudia* [1943].

Choosing the Enemy
Origins and Contents of Films
Shown in France and the United States in 1939

	Pacifist	Anti-Japan-ese	Anti-German or anti-Nazi	Soviet	Anti-Soviet	German films	Italian films[b]
France (of 250 films, 100 were widely distributed)	2[A]	0	2	1	1	0	1
United States (of 500 films, 150 were widely distributed)	2	1[B]	18[D]	16[E]	2[C]	9[a]	4

a. None of these German films received important reviews either in the *New York Times* or in other major papers: none was seen in major Broadway houses. Among them one notes: *Drei Unteroffiziere* [Werner Hochbaum, 1939], *Der Florentiner* [Hut Wolfgang Liebeneiner, 1939], *Der Gouverneur* [Victor Tourjansky, 1939].
b. *Scipione l'Africano* [Carmine Gallone, 1937], *Il grande appello* [Mario Camerini, 1936], *Ho perduto mio marito* [Enrico Guarroni, 1937], *Allegri Masnadieri* [Marco Elter, 1937].
A. *All Quiet On the Western Front* [Lewis Milestone, 1930] (revival), *Entente cordiale*.
B. *Flight Angels* [Lewis Seiler, 1940].
C. *Ninotchka, Sky Patrol*.
D. *Beasts of Berlin* [Shennan Scott, 1939], *U-Boat 29* [Michael Powell, 1939], *Conspiracy* [Lew Landers, 1939], *They Made Her a Spy* [Jack Hively, 1939], etc.
E. *The Oppenheims, Swamp Soldiers, A Great Citizen*.

d) Films made to justify the pact with the Soviets (*Mission to Moscow* [Michael Curtiz, 1943], *The North Star* [Lewis Milestone, 1943]), which can be contrasted with anti-Soviet films.

e) Films produced between 1939 and 1944, made by Hollywood's ex-"Communists" and attacked by the McCarthy subcommittee or by pacifist-isolationist organizations such as the Knights of Columbus: William Dieterle's *Blockade* [1938], Mervyn LeRoy's *Escape*, Frank Borzage's *Three Comrades*, Irving Pichel's *The Man I Married*, Anatole Litvak's *Confessions of a Nazi Spy*, Archie Mayo's *Four Sons*, and Frank Borzage's *The Mortal Storm*.

American films on Nazism[1] have certain things in common:
—The German people are always disassociated from the regime which exerts its power only over adolescents and/or inexperienced people.

—They overvalue the German people's will as well as their capacity to resist Nazism.

—The action always takes place in small or midsized towns.

—The way terror functions and its connections to the system are described from within, in a way even very few novels achieve. The outer forms of political life and the history of Nazism itself play an important role only in documentaries.

—In fictional films the triumph of Nazism results in the rupture of good relations within families and among neighbors.

In the great majority of films about American society and the war, family life is precisely "the unconquered fortress" which becomes stronger than ever. The story of a wife who faithfully awaits her husband's return constitutes the secondary theme in almost all the films and the principal theme in a good number. Maintaining friendly, neighborly feelings is what constitutes an indication of the group's moral health. In *Visions of Yesterday* (London: Routledge & Kegan Paul, 1973), Jeffrey Richards has correctly observed that, as an image of the American ideal, life in a small town has replaced the life of pioneers and *yeoman*. It has been transcribed to the present era as the embodiment of an ideal opposed to that underlying *big business*, the "machinery" of political parties, or the state. Good relations among neighbors—the only modern alternative to *self-help*—are the foundation and the sign of American liberties. In Germany Nazism destroyed these relationships of trust, as well as those of the family (that other cornerstone of American society).

The other principal theme of *anti-Japanese* films is simple. There are no values other than those defended by American democracy. The enemy's only chance for salvation is to share these values, and from the moment he does so he ceases to be an enemy.

A perfect example of this occurs in *Behind the Rising Sun*. The young Nipponese who returns to his country in 1937 after studying in the United States is completely Americanized. His eyes opened, he discovers with amazement the real meaning of

American liberties. Although his father is a liberal anti-militarist deputy, he nevertheless wants to force him into a profession that has been chosen for him. This is unlike the United States where each person freely chooses for himself. His family also wants to choose a wife from a "good family" for him even though he loves his father's young secretary.

The Sino-Japanese war breaks out to the despair of the family which, although clearly divided, is also human and pacifist. Enrolled in the Japanese army the young hero deteriorates and decays. Converted into a "true soldier of the Mikado," he closes his eyes to the horrors committed in China. Successively, he loses his love for truth, his freedom of judgment, and even his feelings of fidelity toward the young girl he has promised to marry. He becomes a torturer, a real monster. His father, who has remained a traditionalist but is still liberal and tolerant, commits suicide in despair while the young girl thanks heaven when she hears the first American bomber planes going over her country bringing liberty.

Although hostility to the Soviets was never as deeply rooted in the United States as in Great Britain or France, a great leap had to be made to present Americans with a favorable image of the U.S.S.R. In their first two productions concerning this issue Warner Brothers went all out.

In *Mission to Moscow*, what counts is not so much the solemn tone or the bombast of this reportage inspired by Ambassador Davies's *Memoires*. The depiction of the Soviet Union is limited to a few edifying scenes dealing with the mechanization of agriculture, the spectacular transformation of tractors into tanks, and the social emancipation of women (one of the most developed themes). Good intentions constitute the whole framework of this film which tries, in less than two hours, to disarm every suspicion concerning the Stalinist regime. "Our form of government is the best possible in the world," Ambassador Davies remarks, "but I respect the honesty of the Soviet leaders." This pithy "but" leads into a long passage justifying the Stalinist purges of the 1930s—a passage which, incidentally, does not appear in this form in Davies's *Memoires*. Trotskyites tried in vain to deny the truth of this passage. And in fact *as depicted by Hollywood*, the presentation of these trials was enough to make them choke with impotent anger. At a cocktail party Litvinov mysteriously tells an American about traitors who exist in his country. Alternating shots then depict an act of sabotage at Kharkov where oil wells go up in flames and the arrest soon afterward of Krestinsky, Radek, and Bukharin, as well as shots of Nazis committing similar acts of sabotage in New York. At the time of the trial Yagoda confesses that "their program was inspired by Trotsky" and that "our only hope for success lay in defeating Russia before Germany." Bukharin adds "and Japan" to this while Tukhachevsky concludes, "With Germany's help we planned to establish a military dictatorship and, in order to do so, first Stalin had to be killed." As soon as the trial is over Soviet planes can finally take off.

Unlike this very "historical" film, *The North Star* [1943] (with Anne Baxter) is designed to entertain and leave a pleasant memory of Soviet life. In fact the little Ukrainian town it depicts is a true paradise, and were it not for the samovars and braids we could well be in the Midwest. It is filled with more ducks, suckling pigs and other food—in short, a real picnic—than could be found in all the markets of Moscow. At home, the husband is so affectionate, the wife so attached to her home, the children so well brought up, and the young so well behaved, that it's hard to imagine that the Soviets could be jealous of anything in America. It is easy to understand why the McCarthy subcommittee could consider *The North Star* a subversive film once the war was over. In fact, the only explicit moral of this simpering work by Lewis Milestone—which also depicts Soviet men as brave, patriotic, loyal, and resolute in the face of a German surprise attack in the midst of a celebration—is that the more cultivated the Germans (with Erich von Stroheim playing a Nazi doctor) the more they are guilty of the crimes they commit.

(1974)

NOTES

1. Cf. Edward Dmytryk's *Hitler's Children* (1942); Fred Zinnemann's *The Seventh Cross* (1944); Irving Pichel's *The Man I Married*, Peter Godfrey's *Hotel Berlin* (1945); Henry Hathaway's *The House on 92nd Street* (1945); Herman Shumlin's *Watch on the Rhine* (1943); and Anatole Litvak's *Confessions of a Nazi Spy*.

117

CHAPTER 9

Does an Anti-militarist Cinema Exist?

It would seem that a great many anti-militarist films exist, from Georges Meliès's *L'Affaire Dreyfus* [1899] to *Gardarem lo Larzac* [Dr. Bloch, P. Haudiquet, I. Levy, 1974]. But the truth is that these films, which are often parodies or simply marginal, tackle the faults of militarism and the military spirit, as well as the absurdity and naïveté of military dogmas. They show how applying military precepts may lead to tragic or absurd situations involving suicide, death, and defeat. This is the lesson found in *Mädchen In Uniform* [Leontine Sagan, 1931], in Max Ophüls's *Liebelei* [1933], and in a more cheerful vein in American comedies of the 1920s or in *The Bridge on the River Kwai* [David Lean, 1957]. As for French cinema it abounds in Courteline-type farces.

Another tradition exists which condemns the excesses of military discipline. From *All Quiet on the Western Front* to *Attack!* [Robert Aldrich, 1956] and *From Here to Eternity* [Zinnemann, 1953], it analyzes the military institution and its functioning in a more direct manner. In their time these films had an impact upon the public. They attacked taboos in those

118

countries which successively played the role of counterrevolutionary policeman—Germany of the 1930s and post-World
War II America. They clearly show the abuses authorized by
military discipline and the practices it allows. All the same, this
group of films does not expose the basic problem of militarism
nor even that of the military institution. If we examine the way in
which these films present *individual* hazings and the latitude left
to those in charge, we see that they do not tackle the essential
problem, which involves the social function of the military institution and its repressive role as far as political conflicts and collective struggles are concerned.

The same is true of a whole series of famous films—in the
vein of *J'accuse*—like *Three Comrades, Okraina, Uomini contro*
[Francesco Rosi, 1970], *Paths of Glory* [Stanley Kubrick, 1957],
and *King and Country* [Joseph Losey, 1964]. These films intermingle the theme of anti-militarism and that of *pacifism* in a
confused way. As far as the last two films are concerned, Losey's,
which is more recent, goes one step further than Kubrick's in
analyzing the military institution. Let us see why this is so. On
the surface *Paths of Glory* involves all the themes of World War I
and post–World War I anti-militarism. The motives behind the
1916 offensive-at-any-price are made clearly explicit and are
probed from the top to the bottom of the military hierarchy. The
arbitrariness of military justice is also laid bare when the three
soldiers are condemned to death and executed in order to cover
up the abuses and errors of those in command. An inexpiable
attack against the military institution, this film "pleases" liberals
and left-wingers. The way the film heaps up extreme situations
(even if, taken singly, each situation is authentic) and intermingles them neutralizes the credibility of its overall viewpoint. It
also makes it hard to understand the birth and long life of veter-
ans' organizations where—for many years after the war—soldiers
and officers continued to fraternize with each other.

King and Country

Joseph Losey's less spectacular analysis goes further and gets
closer to the central problem. The action takes place in 1917 in
the trenches of Flanders. The soldier Hamp, who enlisted as a

volunteer to "teach his mother-in-law something," has been fighting courageously for three years. All of his fellow soldiers have died. On the day of a cannonade he "cracks" and to flee the cannon's noise he starts to walk, leaves the lines, and—without really realizing it—he "deserts." "It's the first time that that happened to me," he says in his defense before the military tribunal who believes him and understands that they are dealing with a simple man who does not know the subtleties of the regulations and their deep implications. Nonetheless, obedience to the military code gets the better of justice and the tribunal condemns him. Since the attack is scheduled for the next day, the command orders an immediate execution for "King and country."

The film is interesting in that it deals not with the war itself but with the distance which separates the law (and the knowledge of law) from the common people who are ill-informed, badly trained, scarcely educated, and defenseless in the face of institutions (in this case, the military establishment). No one is supposed to be ignorant of the law, but everything is arranged so that the people do not understand it and remain in ignorance. If they knew it they would be able to grasp how it originated, reasoned, and functioned.

If it is true that war and the state of war help the military to seize its turn at power and thereby realize its true ambitions, they also help us to catch the institution in flagrante delicto. Nonetheless, you can see the *permanent* function of the army in a more pertinent way if the war is not a patriotic one but rather a civil war. This is why the films of René Vautier are interesting. *Avoir vingt ans dans les Aurès* [1971], notably, examines the problem of corps solidarity between soldiers and officers. The study of the inner functioning of the military goes deeper here because, instead of intermingling with pacificism, anti-militarism intermingles with a political struggle which is relevant today. Rosa Luxemburg wrote, "The immaturity of the masses will be in evidence as long as soldiers let themselves be abused by their officers." She raised a problem which continues to divide anti-militarists. If it is true that the army has a twofold function that involves repression as well as patriotism, it is also certain that, deprived of the officers' experience and knowledge, soldiers will not be able to understand how the institution sets about diverting military discipline from its original function—the amelioration of combat capacity—in order to use it as a means of social repression. Contemporary militant films bear witness to this.[1] But none has yet shown how the mechanism really works.[2]

(1976)

NOTES

1. A list of contemporary anti-militarist films can be found in Guy Hennebelle's *Le Cinéma militant* (Paris: Film édition/Pierre L'herminier, 1976).

2. Except for Russian soldiers and officers during the Revolution of 1917. Cf. my *The Russian Revolution of February 1917*.

SOCIETY WHICH PRODUCES,
SOCIETY WHICH RECEIVES

CHAPTER 10

Conflict Within *The Third Man*

When it came out in 1949, Sir Carol Reed's *The Third Man* received an icy critical welcome. "Grandiloquent and overblown mise-en-scène" wrote Georges Sadoul; while in the United States Bosley Crowther, the well-known critic of the *New York Times*, deemed it "a film without social reality or significance. A plot concerning the black market is not of the slightest interest. The film is no more than a melodrama full of tricks." These observations were soon refuted by a *grand prix* at the Venice festival and then by twenty-five years of success. Nonetheless, the gap between early critical reactions and popular approval creates a problem, even more so because the film's release was also accompanied by much hullabaloo: the zither of Anton Karas, an unknown musician Carol Reed heard playing by chance while he was out scouting in the Vienna streets; the "location" shooting in the "liberated" Austrian capital which was half in ruins; and the contribution of Orson Welles, who improvised his lines about the Italy of the condottieri, Switzerland, and the cuckoo clock. With total seriousness these critics first went into details concerning Orson Welles's fear of developing bronchitis while shooting in the Viennese sewers, and then said that he was so fascinated by these scenes that he had them lengthened. This list gives us a good idea of the parade of publicity anecdotes with which critics often like to accompany the production of a big-budget film.

However, neither Orson Welles's lines, nor the zither, nor the sewers, nor the rubble of Vienna reveals what *The Third Man* is about. The film is a political tragedy written in the spirit of the Cold War and it is violently anti-Communist. All the same, the violence of the positions it takes is not always clear because its politics are hidden behind a much deeper mythic plot which alludes—as only Bardèche has seen—to the myth of Antigone and because this work (situated at the crossroads of ideas coming from Arthur Koestler, Albert Camus, and Christian humanism) expressed the ideological antagonisms separating Graham Greene (author of the scenario), Orson Welles, and Carol Reed (the film's director) from each other. It is this conflict that we want to examine.

The author of the scenario had a very different conception of the film at the beginning. Greene had written, and had wanted to write, something to "entertain." Carol Reed's direction "deeply disappointed" him. Greene was won over to it only much later when *The Third Man* became a world-wide success.

As Léna Grigoriadou has observed, one of the film's dramatic impulses springs very much from its perpetual changes in orientation that modify the way the viewer identifies with the film's heroes. At the beginning no hero is defined; then the narrator's voice-over (which is that of Carol Reed) disappears suddenly after having presented Vienna to us. From then on the viewer follows the trail of Rollo (Holly) Martins, the hero who has been introduced in the voice-over and who is conducting an inquiry into his friend's unexpected death. A straightforward hero, he is rendered even more immediately likeable through the clear contrast between him and the other characters we meet at the beginning of the film. Calloway, in charge of the English military police, is alternatively arrogant, somewhat slow, discourteous, and unpolished; the organizer of the Cultural Centre is bustling and crude; the Baron Kurz is carefully rendered suspicious and disloyal by the camera; Anna is presented at the beginning as a frivolous little actress who is indifferent to her friend's death and constantly involved in little details and in her success. In her case a pronounced displacement takes place in respect to the scenario where these traits are hardly noticeable.

Later on, through successive touches, Holly's personality loses in consistency, and its purity corrodes. He immediately falls for his best friend's companion, and, in order to protect her from the Soviet police, he denounces and sells out the friend he has just found once again. This bargain does not appear in Greene's script. Preferring the laws of the state to natural laws, when Holly learns that Harry Lime (his best friend, a childhood friend) has become a criminal who traffics in penicillin, he sells him to the police in exchange for the liberty of his woman. But Anna, a modern Antigone, refuses this pact and demonstrates intransigent rectitude. Her beloved may have been a criminal but she still is one with him and has nothing but scorn for the man who now courts her. This first reversal is followed by a second one. By the end of the film the policeman has taken on a certain consistency. He pursues a criminal for whom he feels quite simply a tenacious hatred—he does what he must. Although he negotiates with Holly to exchange Anna's freedom for the capture of the third man, he treats Holly merely with condescending indifference whereas he admires the young woman's resolute character. At the end of the film, when Lime dies in the sewer finished off by his friend, it is not the policeman who should feel guilty.

While these psychological reversals do not appear in the scenario, Reed's realization takes us far from the "entertainment" that Greene had in mind. Certainly the Christian moralist wanted to raise the problem running throughout his work: there is no "positive" hero since good and evil are mixed in each one of us. Neither Holly nor Harry is completely good nor completely evil. Besides, *The Third Man* makes us ask ourselves whether or not a man who has admired another man all his life (as Holly has admired Harry) must hand him over to the police. The script grazes over these problems: "My only intention was to amuse, to make people laugh. I didn't intend to provoke political senti-ments." But Carol Reed *did* want to provoke them, and he politi-cized the film. He increased its weightiness and its documentary significance by adding two sequences—which have *the filmic form of a documentary*—on the harm done by bootleg penicillin. Above all, he reversed the moral at the end of the film and thereby made Greene so angry that Greene broke off all relations with the director. In fact, in the script, when the long traveling shot shows Anna coming back from the cemetery where Harry has just been buried, Holly is waiting for her—she joins him and they leave together. "That's the way life is. Men and women wind up together," comments Graham Greene. "Not always," responds Reed, who shot the scene his way. Head erect, Alida Valli walks by Holly without a glance—giving the scene a nobility whose beauty Greene acknowledged later on. In this way Reed completed the uncompromising portrait of Antigone. But this contribution went far beyond these important modifications. He also changed the scene of the cafe ambush. In the script Holly is seized with remorse at having prepared a trap for his friend and is reluctant at the last moment to let him be captured. In the film it is Anna who comes to the rendezvous, scents the trap, prowls around, insults the felon Holly and, as soon as Harry appears, gives the signal for alarm. Harry can therefore escape to the sewers. The modified sequence shows us a Holly who has lost all scruples. While Greene wanted Holly's character to be ambiguous, Reed made him into a weak and inconsistent man.

Put together, all of Reed's modifications made Anna into the strong character of the film, a true positive hero. Whereas the script had her as a Hungarian, the daughter of a Nazi, Reed changes her into a Czechoslovakian citizen fleeing the Communist regime. The film was shot just after the Prague coup of 1948. In addition, the Soviet police hides its necessarily criminal activities and, as we have seen, Reed chose the filmic genre of the documentary to add an even stronger sense of truthfulness. Moreover, the police fail in their obligation toward their agent, Harry Lime, by not protecting him. Thus, whoever compromises himself with the Soviets will know only dishonor or death.

The character who symbolizes liberty and rectitude becomes Czech rather than Hungarian; the one who betrays his friend and lacks character (traits emphasized by Sir Carol Reed's contribution) turns out to be an American, whereas the scenario had him as English. This change is linked—and not totally innocently—to a change in the choice of the actor who, at the beginning, was not supposed to be Joseph Cotten. The transformation in Holly appears equally significant because none of his negative traits appeared in the scenario: awkward, inattentive, confusing Calloway and Callagham, Winckel and Vinkel, committing blunders and boners, and thereby revealing that he comes from a country where one can no longer distinguish between an Englishman and an Irishman, or between an Austrian and a Prussian. In short, he behaves—to the eyes of an Englishman—like an American during World War II: restless, naïve, in need of guidance, confusing civilian and military police, the "free" world and the "Communist" world, as if the police of the former did not pursue crime. Here these crimes are committed by the Soviets. They are allies who one must perforce get along with but, at the same time, one must be more wary about them than the Americans were at Yalta.

Thus, as the following diagrams show, the general sense Reed's transformation of the novel (which went against Graham Greene's wishes) expresses—*on the symbolic and latent scene of World War II*—the conflict between an Englishman's conceptions and values and those of a citizen who would like to be above the fray. In fact, a balance sheet of the changes effected by Reed shows that only the English and the Czech citizen are positive heroes. The Americans are inconsistent, frivolous, and irresponsible; the Russians are necessary allies but objective representatives of crime; the Romanians and other Central Europeans are ambiguous and dangerous beings.

All this expresses very well the viewpoint of an Englishman who has experienced the German-Soviet pact,[1] World War II, and America's "incomprehensible weakness" (in the years 1941–44) toward the Communist system. For Reed the only innocent victims here are children and an English policeman.

Pro-English, anti-Soviet, critical of Americans—such is the film that Carol Reed, a jingoist Englishman, made against the wishes of Graham Greene as he *substituted a morality of Good and Evil for a morality of ambiguity*. Henceforth it becomes easy to understand the origin of their quarrel, the reticency of Georges Sadoul (who was a Communist), and of the American critic Bosley Crowther.

But the film involved another conflict, and this one wound

Reed's Transformations in Nationalities

	Graham Greene	Carol Reed
ANNA HOLLY PUPESCU	Hungarian English American (Cooler)	Czech American Romanian

	Positive Heroes	Vacillating Heroes	Negative Heroes
Filmic Scene	ANNA Czech, anti- Communist CALLOWAY English, fights crimi- nals	ROLLO MAR- TINS Clearly American	KURZ Austrian VINKEL Austrian PUPESCU Austrian SOVIET OFFICER
Symbolic scene of World War II	Moral strength, sense of responsibility Deceiving the Soviets is not lying An exorcism of Mu- nich? (Russians=Germans. One wants to save the Czechs but cannot.)	Blind or irresponsible allies Arrival on the Euro- pean scene Physical strength	Duplicity Reminders of the axis: Berlin–Moscow–Bucharest Austrians=Germans

up with the victory of the third man—that is, Orson Welles—at the expense of Carol Reed. Welles shifted the film, creating a *reversal* which, although along the lines desired by Graham Greene, worked to his own advantage, since in the collective memory of many viewers *The Third Man* is the work of Orson Welles.[2]

Thanks to the actor's powerful personality and to his impro-visations and injunctions, Harry Lime becomes—contrary to the wish of the director who wanted him to make a brief appearance—the film's *other* tragic hero. And as such he represents an incarnation of the morality of ambiguity defined by Greene. This one is a modern hero, at once cynical and sensitive, desperate and proud, whose code does not obey the norms of society and who, as Vonnie Ferro suggests, represents the new figure of the adventurer without a country. In fact, the film does not clearly define his nationality. All that defines him is a friend, a woman, a cat. "In any case, I won't harm you," he says to Holly. And although he pretends to mock Holly and says he's not worried about Anna's fate, he hides in order to write her beloved name on the cabin's misty panes. A man of the night, the only one trusted by the cat, his movements are free only when he is underground, away from the gaze of the living. It is there that he waits for Anna, that he lives freely, that he loves and dies.

Orson Welles compelled Carol Reed to lengthen the sewer sequence. Visually, Carol Reed found himself obliged to compensate for, and to announce, this immense black spot at the end of the film. He added two nighttime chases as well as the short sequence with the cat to the thriller plot. All these scenes were shot askew, like Harry Lime's gait or like a baroque set.

The film's double imprint retains its power and evokes—at the level of chiaroscuro contrasts and musical motifs going from major to minor keys—the disquieting ambiguity of a society in which one can no longer believe.[3]

(1976)

NOTES

1. Note that among the "occupiers" only the Russians can speak German and communicate directly with the people.

2. For a majority of viewers, also, the scenes with Orson Welles are those remembered most clearly. This factor cannot really be separated from the way these scenes are created.

3. In the film Anna's role is played by Alida Valli and that of Calloway by Trevor Howard. (On *The Third Man*, see *Literature Film Quarterly*, II, 1974, an issue devoted to Graham Greene's films, notably the contributions of the Rev. Gene D. Phillips and that of J. A. Gomez.)

CHAPTER 11

La grande illusion and Its Receptions

The reception Jean Renoir's *La grande illusion* [*Grand Illusion*] are indicative of French society before and after the war. When the film came out in 1937 the left-wing press greeted *La grande illusion* as a pacifist work that argued in favor of good relations between different peoples.[1] The film showed that the true reality of History did not lie in national conflicts but in the class struggle, and that consequently there was no reason for war to exist. This viewpoint was confirmed by the reactions of Nazi authorities who banned the film because it weakened national spirit, showed Jews in a sympathetic light, and depicted a German woman giving herself to a French prisoner. Later on the actress Dita Parlo was upset about even having accepted the role. However, other reactions to the same film indicate that its content was not unambiguous. Before Goebbels amputated all the scenes where the Jew appears likeable, Göring had welcomed the film. The Socialist minister, Spaak, banned it in Belgium for the same reason that Warner Brothers refused to release it in the United States—it was thought to be too "chauvinistic." Ten years later, hotly criticized by the Resistance press (notably by Georges Altman in *Franc-Tireur*), *La grande illusion* was shown but with several scenes cut, while the scenes cut in 1937 were restored. Let us take another look at some aspects of the film in order to better understand its relationship to the society viewing it [la société réceptrice].

Its very title expressed the director's intentions, which were in line with the interpretation given the film by the left-wing press in 1937. The illusion is grand on the part of those who fought in 1914–18 and who, as Claude Beylie says, "were happy and free only in common suffering." They had the "illusion" that this wartime fraternity tolled the end of social antagonisms. In the first version of the scenario, the aristocratic captain did not die but rather made an appointment with the proletarian lieutenant to meet him at Maxim's after the war. But it was clear that they would never see one another again. With peace restored the class barrier would be reborn and erected higher than ever.

According to histories of cinema, the scenario was modified due to Jean Renoir's meeting with Erich von Stroheim. Fascinated by his personality, Renoir enlarged Stroheim's role, and the relationship between the French officer, Fresnay, and the German officer [Stroheim] became more important. From then on the couple Fresnay-Stroheim balanced the couple Fresnay-Gabin. The initial idea was modified first by the death of the French captain—the only end in keeping with the elevated nature of their relationship. But this change profoundly alters the film's ideology and makes it opaque, for it means that patriotism and death acquire the same weight as internationalism and the class struggle; the gesture of the individual hero begins to become more important than the shared feelings born of common suffering. A discrepancy occurs in going from Spaak's original scenario to Renoir's film. Certainly Renoir declared himself and wanted to be on the Left. His acts bore witness to this. Nonetheless, he remained attached to traditional values. Moreover, as far as the 1914–18 war is concerned, his admiration is won not by crouching and filthy doughboys, but by the individual hero, the chevalier of the skies—the ace pilot. Renoir's happy complicity with his aristocratic heroes is not accidental. Rather, it is explicable in terms of the director's own sentiments: "I had been a cavalry officer; well, the majority of the cavalry officers came from the aristocracy." This complicity is at the core of one of the film's ambiguities and its different receptions. If it is true, as Pierre Sorlin observes, that the film's real hero is in fact the proletarian officer who successfully undergoes a whole series of difficulties as he simultaneously wins both a woman and his liberty, it is also necessary to go along with Sorlin's further observation that this initiation rite is deeply rooted in a traditional ritual having nothing to do with the proletarian, pacifist behavior that could have constituted the narrative's dramatic shell. As he remarks quite correctly, the film's construction, as well as the modifications made in the scenario, invite us to carefully analyze the work's latent content. Let us see what this means in certain respects.

In 1937, at the time of the anti-Semitic campaign directed against Léon Blum and the Popular Front, the film appeared to be a response to the calumnies found in *Gringoire* and the Maurrassian publications.[2] The Jewish Rosenthal did not try to shirk his duty but fought in the war like all Frenchmen. He generously shared the contents of his packages with his fellow prisoners. He also shared their courage. His quarrel with Jean Gabin is a scene of exorcism. Instinctively anti-Semitic, the Frenchman becomes aware of the nature of his impulses which he then dominates, realizing that his anti-Semitism is groundless. In the climate of 1937 this film was fully satisfying to the victims of racism. The anti-Semitic Goebbels was not mistaken when he specifically cut those scenes concerning Jews.

In retrospect the portrayal of the Jews appears in a different light. All the traits attributed to Rosenthal make him into someone who stands apart. He is the only one to receive packages and mail and the only one able to distribute cigarettes. He speaks of defending his country in order to save his possessions and brags about having a family that became richer in one generation—his patriotism is far from unselfish. The changes brought about in the dialogues vie with one another in their anti-Semitism. A gibe made by a soldier in the first version—"Him, an athlete, he was born in Jerusalem"—later becomes, "Your country, you don't have one, you were born in Jerusalem." A joke made by a prisoner—"After all, he's from old Breton nobility"—revives a polemical debate of 1936: "Is a Jew worth a Breton?" Finally (in a scene cut after the war) when Rosenthal gives some chocolate to a German sentry, another prisoner comments, "Everything's rotten." For him, as for the spectator, it is the Jew who collaborates with the Germans while the aristocratic captain, always aloof, refuses von Rauffenstein's overtures. A final sentence reveals the depths of anti-Semitism in France: "I'm beginning to get used to Rosenthal's kindnesses," comments a teacher as the dialogue reveals an astonishing complicity with the society producing it.

The observations concerning the Germans and the English are equally indicative of the film's latent ideology. The Germans are portrayed as men who are moved by a genuine humanity. The sentry says "bonsoir" to the prisoners; the jailor offers his harmonica to Maréchal; the German women pity the young men who are training before leaving for the front; and von Rauffenstein exhibits humor and nobility. "The jailors are honest," observes the teacher, thus rehearsing before 1940 what the French were to say of the Germans during the first months of the occupation.

The scenes where the English appear show them to advantage only once—when they interrupt their costume show, take off their wigs, and stand at attention in order to sing the *Marseillaise* and celebrate the victory at Verdun. All the other instances are negative—the arrival of the English prisoners with their tennis rackets (for them, war is like a game; they are not "real" soldiers); the total absence of communication with the English (while there is some with the Russians); and their implied homosexuality (unlike the virile Frenchman who "screws" at the beginning and the end of the film). A characteristic example: The aristocratic Boeldieu—who uses the English language as an aristocratic code to converse with von Rauffenstein—"forgets" that he knows English when he should tell his English companions, who are allies and former prisoners, that a tunnel has been dug under the barracks. But the French ask themselves whether they should confide this secret to the English or not, as if an Englishman were not an ally—or as if he were not a sure ally. This ambiguity is revealing, especially since it occurs three years before Vichy. Other elements appear in the film which, without the director's knowledge or desire, make it into a perfect model of a virtual apology in favor of Vichy: hostility and scorn toward intellectuals (on the part of the French as well as the Germans), and resentment against women who, flighty and immoral, do not respect family values.

In 1946, by a rather extraordinary shift in interpretation, the film was seen as an invitation to accept collaboration and all its clichés. Jean Renoir then cut the love scene with Dita Parlo that Goebbels (for different reasons) also wanted to cut. In 1946 this scene seemed to depict the image of the "good" German woman as well as that of the Frenchman on the make—two intolerable images coming right after the Occupation and the Resistance. In 1937 Jean Renoir had already cut some lines of Boeldieu who, upon hearing the stamp of German soldiers, says: "The noise of marching is the same in all the armies of the world." In 1946 this last breath of internationalism became inadmissable because the comparison between the French and the Nazi boot was unacceptable. It was already inadmissable in 1937 when the defeat announced by the film (France is conquered and only the resourceful Frenchman triumphs) gave the French the foreboding that the German boot even at that date represented something more than an army. In the film Renoir's good internationalist intentions retain hardly any reality or substance.

These observations concerning *La grande illusion* are incomplete; they concern solely the ways the film relates to the society producing and receiving it. A whole series of problems—such as the depiction of the Great War, the film's construction, the treatment of actors, the choice of sets, the relationships of the shots—have not been examined. The only goal of these observations was to show what could be gained simply from information concerning the film's reception in two different eras.

(1974–75)

NOTES

1. We express our thanks to Jacques Cleynen who graciously showed us his documentation on *La grande illusion*.

2. [Translator's note: Charles Maurras was a right-wing, pro-monarchist French writer who helped found the reactionary journal *L'action française* in 1908. During World War II he was an ardent defender of the Vichy government and was condemned for collaboration in 1945. *Gringoire* was a major right-wing newspaper in the 1930s. Its film reviewer was Georges Champeaux.]

MODES OF ACTION OF
CINEMATOGRAPHIC LANGUAGE

CHAPTER 12

Dissolves in *Jud Süss*

The success of *Jud Süss* [Veidt Harlan, 1940] is well known, as is the part Goebbels played in its realization and the tragic destiny that later awaited most of those who had worked on it. It is also known that the film-maker, Veidt Harlan, always denied having wanted to make an anti-Semitic film and that he enlisted in the Wehrmacht in order not to be in charge of the film when he was asked to make it. According to him he accepted an assignment to make a historical film *on* the Jewish problem. He maintained that Goebbels was angry that Harlan succeeded in eliminating certain scenes (which Goebbels desired) because their connotation was too obvious. At his trial in 1945, he maintained his good faith, showed his proofs, and American justice condemned him to a light sentence.

Whoever has seen the film knows full well that this argument does not hold up under analysis. In a 1979 *Annales* article, François Garçon, in collaboration with D. J. Jay and Michel Pierre, has shown that in fact several readings of *Jud Süss* exist and that even if the film's inspiration is also anti-feminist, petit bourgeois, and rather rigorously Hitlerian, this does not take away from the perfect coherence of its anti-Semitism. The film combines several strata of anti-Semitism. The fact that the most frequent of these is the least noticeable is what allowed Veidt Harlan to sway some of his judges.

Garçon's fine article confines itself to the level of what is explicit. I would like to corroborate its viewpoint by analyzing one aspect of the film's realization (an aspect which bears on cinematic writing) in order to use a concrete example to show that ideology exists at the level of filmic writing and the "purely" technical way that the camera is used. In this instance we are dealing with the technique called a dissolve (a rather subtle exercise of going from one shot to another). This effect could be deemed recherché since it requires special handling between the editing and the printing.

There are four dissolves in *Jud Süss*. The first: when the camera leaves the ducal emblem that is affixed to the chateau and goes to the Hebrew emblem that is attached to a store in the ghetto. The dissolve is used to go from the chateau to the Jewish neighborhood. The second: when Süss shaves his beard for his visit to the Duke. The dissolve shows the transformation in his face and attire. The third: when Süss tosses onto the Duke's desk the gold pieces that metamorphose into graceful ballerinas. The fourth: when a condemned and imprisoned Süss once more looks like his old self after his beard grows in prison.

What these four effects imply is not innocent. The Jew has two faces: his ghetto face (which does not lie about his subhuman nature), and his city face (which is no less harmful despite its deceptive appearance). By the utilization of gold, of which he is a past master, the Jew introduces into the chateau the taste for lucre, a taste intimately linked to debauchery. He perverts a society which was healthy and thereby harms the health of the race. The change from one escutcheon to another symbolizes the passage of power from Aryans to Jews.

Thus, the decision to use these dissolves assumes an ideological significance because, when seen and analyzed as a group, these four effects constitute a structure, a summary of Nazi doctrine. Consciously or not, the filmmaker identified the elements defining the essence of Nazi doctrine and reserved the film's only special effects for them. In some way, then, Veidt Harlan's art betrayed him.

(1976)

CHAPTER 13

Interviews in the Works of Ophüls, Harris, and Sédouy

In the history of the film documentary *Le chagrin et la pitié* represents a kind of October Revolution. By its repercussions (which were clearly linked to its theme) and its orientation, this work, done by Marcel Ophüls in collaboration with André Harris and Alain de Sédouy, evokes a feeling whose meaning varies according to the viewer's ideology, but which always goes beyond the bounds of reactions usually evoked by a cinematographic work.

In many ways its success also comes from the exceptional qualities of the film's realization. I do not know if this has been sufficiently noted. Its makers experimented in a new way with an old device—the use of interviews. In *Le chagrin et la pitié*, just as later in *Français, si vous saviez* by André Harris and Alain de Sédouy [1972–73], interviews have a twofold role and a new function.

The role of the interview is to confront a character from the present with his own past, as in the interview with Marius Klein, the Clermont-Ferrand merchant. When he is interviewed this witness is asked about Jewish merchants in his neighborhood. He appears unconcerned by these unhappy memories, a little as if he had not known about all that at the time—as if this drama had been simply a part of the misfortunes of war. This witness has a last name which could be misleading. When the interviewer shows Klein a notice that he placed in the newspapers in 1941 to make it clear that he was not Jewish, Klein blanches and can say only: "Ah! So you knew that." In one stroke the viewer can see the cowardice and weakness of this character who thereby recreates precisely the climate of 1941.

The interview confronts the witness's image of the past with the reality. When the former bicycle racer Raphael Geminiani, who has become a bartender, declares that there were no Germans in Clermont-Ferrand, we see a shot of him and then, as his observations are heard in voice-over the filmmaker gives us shots of Germans marching or walking about in Clermont-Ferrand.

The testimony of individuals in this film functions, above all, to replace the commentary which often gives way to questions asked of witnesses and/or to the synchronous commentary of newsreels of that era. Ophüls (with Sédouy in the interviews) never resorts to a traditional sort of commentary. Thus, the historian outwardly effaces himself in favor of his witnesses, of society, of the testimony of the past. In the absence of this mediation the historical explanation appears terribly authentic, as if endowed with an additional measure of truth.

This way of writing or structuring a film gives it its force whether the viewer agrees or disagrees with its orientation. Whereas the force of images in a film is traditionally stronger than the text, the contrary is true this time thanks to a new system of relations linking the text, the oral discourse, and the discourse of images. The almost total lack of music even goes unnoticed. The truth is that the divergent ideologies of the film's authors led to a choice of witnesses who, playing off each other, were to constitute a sort of national sample. In order to be effective, any critique of this choice should deal not only with the depiction or the ideology of the different categories of witnesses (for example, no workers were interviewed, the collaborator had an important role) but with the *energy* radiating from the different witnesses and with their function in the film. It should be noted that while the "collaborator" had ample space, a strong personality, culture, and self-control—all of which are positive qualities—the same was not true of the members of the Resistance. Like the farmers who found it awkward to deal with concepts, or the homosexual parachutist, they possessed less obvious virtues in the eyes of popular morality. All the same since there were counterweights—such as Mendès-France's long testimony (even if all he did was describe events) or Duclos's strong presence and very "negative" evidence about Laval—the film's brilliance rendered its deepest ideology opaque. This ambiguity, together with the high quality of its realization, succeeded rather well in camouflaging the thread of the work and the exploitative principle of the interviews. On the other hand, this exploitative principle was clearly displayed in Harris and Sédouy's second film (made without Ophüls), *Français, si vous saviez.*

Let us examine the choice of witnesses, the nature of the questions asked, the selection of responses, and the editing of these interviews in the latter film.

As the most visible part of the film's explicit and supposed ideology, the choice of witnesses apparently seeks to create a national sample, to be "objective": Pierre Boutang for the extreme Right, Mendès-France for the Left, Duclos and Charles Tillon for the Communists. This balance is neutralized by the editing. While Mendès-France certainly contributes to the film's structure, its architects give it the form they desire through the editing. Hence, it is Pierre Boutang who draws a conclusion from the facts put forth by Mendès-France, thereby reducing the latter to being no more than a chronicler. The Right has the "last word" every time.

The nature of the questions asked is clearly what gives the film its desired meaning. The film settles its account with de Gaulle. In order to do so effectively the authors have shown all the *various anti-Gaullist strata in society:* victims of the Liberation, disappointed Resistance fighters, Algerian repatriots. And the answers are deliberately elicited to such a degree that Soustelle himself, who cannot be accused of having a soft spot for de Gaulle, winds up defending him.

The selection of answers is more difficult to analyze because we do not know what parts of the interviews were used or not. Nonetheless, two anomalies are striking. As far as Daladier is concerned, the editing limits his comments on Munich to his memories concerning how Mussolini and Hitler used to dress. This reveals an obvious desire to discredit still further the former president of the Council, given that Daladier explained himself many, many times about Munich in political terms. Limiting his observations to how the Axis leaders used to dress is part of the global effort to discredit all the political leaders of the Third Republic.

Secondly, the length of the interview with Argoud might surprise people and lead them to conclude, for example, that the authors of *Français, si vous saviez* are right-wingers. In fact, this interview raises questions concerning the narrowness of Argoud's views, and the nature of the political and social system which entrusts heavy responsibilities to such a paranoiac. This testimony could also embarrass the military. But that matters little to film-makers who succeed in showing that they are neither on the Left nor on the Right. Explicit or latent, their aim is a different one. By letting Argoud speak at length, the viewer is led to decide that such a man would not know how to lie and that, consequently, it is de Gaulle who is lying and who has always lied. This implicit conclusion runs throughout the film. De Gaulle lies, as do all political men (Mendès-France is not interviewed about his political activities, but as an individual and a witness), because Truth resides in structures and permanence. The choice of a province as traditional as Lorraine at the beginning of the film clearly denotes the film's anti-political or anti-politician approach.

(1973)

CHAPTER 14

Cinema and Historical Consciousness
in the United States

What historical consciousness does cinema express in the United States? The question is that much more pertinent given that film has played an essential role in the social and cultural life of that country, and that throughout a long era when emigrants from all over still could not speak English well, silent film was able to offer everyone shows and performances accessible to every kind of public.

The problem is whether or not film presents the same representations of the past, and its links with the present, as those found in written historical discourses—tales, scholarly manuals, and novels. It can be noted that the great visions reflected in film transfigure (but with variable modifications) those representations which have successively dominated American life—a life, in fact, which has been dominated by varying, overlapping visions of history superimposed one over the other. Have films, contemporaneously or not, followed this same trajectory? In the United States the *first stratum of* visions of history—which precedes the appearance of cinema—carries the imprint of Christian ideology but, appropriately, of Protestant ideology. In the first history

146

books written in the United States—such as the anonymous *History of the United States of America by a citizen of Massachusetts* (Keene, N.H.: J. Prentiss, 1823)—the accent is put on the superiority of Protestant America compared to Spanish America. The backwardness of Spanish America is attributed "to the superstition and ignorance of its clergy." The proof of the superiority of the Protestant North over Catholic Peru is that "Philadelphia already has twice the number of inhabitants of Lima which was founded 150 years earlier." The book's author even caculates that the United States will have 462,752,896 inhabitants . . . in 1960. He explains that the United States will soon be a paradise because the Yankees are constructing it with the "sweat of their brow." As one can see, history and myth are already linked together. Spain and Catholicism represent what is archaic and evil.

This anti-Spanish tradition is found again in a whole series of films—those with corsairs where the action takes place in Florida, as in *Distant Drums* [Raoul Walsh, 1951]. Their prototypes go back to the early days of cinema. One of the most famous was doubtlessly Michael Curtiz's *The Sea Hawk* [1940] with Errol Flynn. Made during the 1940s, *The Sea Hawk* takes place during the era of Queen Elizabeth I and depicts the Anglo-Saxons as open and likeable, while the Spanish are cruel, pious, and incompetent. One detail bespeaks a kind of slip: Errol Flynn, playing Captain Thorpe, proudly says to the Infanta of Spain, "You have stolen all these jewels from the Indians." A second element of this representation of the past is thus this identification with the English, even though liberty had to be won from them. In fact films evoking the American Revolution are rare even though the number of those evoking the Civil War seems to be infinite.

The ideology of the Civil War constitutes in fact the *second stratum* of the vision of the past. Born at the end of the nineteenth century, this stratum rapidly and definitively took precedence over the previous one. At the point where the nineteenth and twentieth centuries met, two visions of history and politics contrasted violently with each other. It can be observed that D. W. Griffith, who belongs to this generation, justifies [religious] tolerance in *Intolerance* [1916] during an era where there are hundreds of films either for or against tolerance. Some were for the Spanish-American War, others against it; some were for the

Yankees or for the South. From this point of view a 1903 film, Thomas Alva Edison's *Uncle Tom's Cabin*, is significant. Using the themes of Harriet Beecher Stowe's famous novel, the film shows the old domestic in heaven meeting his little mistress, Eva, whom he missed so much. Transformed into an angel she witnesses the great moments which *divided* Americans: Jefferson against Hamilton, the War of 1812, Lincoln and John Wilkes Booth. In other films, such as *In Old Kentucky* [D. W. Griffith, 1909], *Barbara Frietchie* [Metro, 1915], and *The Coward* [Reginald Barker, 1915], American historical conflicts constitute the object of the film. These are films of indictment—sometimes taking one side, sometimes the other.

After World War I hardly any of these films of indictment concern past history. From that point on when an issue arises, it concerns only the present. The transition from the ideology of the Civil War to the ideology of the melting pot (which corresponds to the *third stratum*) is discerned in the films and writings devoted, in fact, to the Civil War. Up to that point the causes of the war and the issues behind the quarrel were emphasized. From that point on it is the effects of the Civil War which are seen as disastrous for the whole country. In this way the Civil War becomes, in some sense, the founding event in the history of the United States, on its way to erasing what preceded it—in particular the American Revolution. In film blacks thus disappear as such from the overall history. They are present only in musicals or novels. Indians, on the contrary, though ignored by written historiography, make a massive appearance in films.

During this period of transition films about the Civil War which directly confront real antagonisms constitute commercial failures—for example, *The Crisis* [1915] by Selig and Churchill. *So Red the Rose* [1935], which expresses the resentment of the whites against Lincoln, was also a failure even though it was by King Vidor. A similar film about this issue, *The Red Badge of Courage* [John Huston, 1951], was also a commercial failure in the 1950s.

The only film which touched upon historically delicate problems and which was a success was *Gone With the Wind* [Victor Fleming, 1939]. But let us note that this film did not depict *any* of the major protagonists of the Civil War—neither

Lincoln nor Lee. No true battle was reconstructed, and while dramatic events of the war—such as the burning of Atlanta—are evoked, it is to condemn war as such rather than to blame one of the two sides. It is a work of national reconciliation, where all the political angles are erased in favor of individual heros, like Scarlett O'Hara or Rhett Butler, who do not incarnate any particular political ideal. Another major approach in this depiction of the past concerns the harmonious integration of immigrants, accompanied by the conquest and then the development of the Middle West and West. King Vidor's *An American Romance* [1944] is the very embodiment of these edifying films.

Thus this *third stratum* is at once that of the ideology of the melting pot and of national reconciliation. *Gone With the Wind* and *An American Romance* incarnate this spirit. During this period, which is born with the United States' entry into war in 1917, all criticism and questioning of the past (even more) than of the present become "un-American." John Ford admirably represents this conformist vision of history where all American institutions are glorified: the armed forces in *Fort Apache* [1948], the traditional family in *How Green Was My Valley* [1941] (even if the action takes place in Ireland) and the triumph of law over lawlessness in *The Man Who Shot Liberty Valence* [1962]. Even if *Young Mr. Lincoln* [1939], a sort of panegyric to the Union-preserving hero, is a totally apolitical film, this is no more than a paradox. In Ford's work only *The Grapes of Wrath* [1940] poses problems concerning American society, but the problems are those of the present and the responsibility for them rests on the 1929 stock market crash rather than on the American leadership. As for gangsters, and the films their appearance gave rise to, they owe their existence only to Prohibition and unemployment. This conformist spirit even extends to other countries when they are depicted. For example, Sam Wood's film on the Spanish Civil War, *For Whom the Bell Tolls* [1943], succeeds in being sympathetic to both Republicans and fascists even though it is taken from Hemingway's novel. Films on Nazism or Communism reconcile themselves with regimes that they condemn by giving the story the form of a comedy; one thinks of Lubitsch's films *Ninotchka* and *To Be or Not to Be* [1942]. Great historical events of the past can be amply recuperated by American society because producers empty them of any allusions which *could divide* Americans. Cecil B. de Mille's *The Ten Commandments* [1956] praises the liberation of the Jews; *Ben Hur* [William Wyler, 1959] and *Quo Vadis* [Mervyn LeRoy, 1951] glorify the birth of Christianity.

Of course there were some protestors among those who wrote history, but more among those who made films about society. Not everyone wrote a history without history. There were some who pointed right to the enemy, though it was never an enemy from within. There were those who condemned what menaced America. The threat of Orientals, the Yellow Peril, was part of a long tradition which begins with anti-Chinese films (around 1927), in an era when China incarnated a Communist revolution (at that time the Japanese represented order and progress). This anti-Oriental tradition, which changed its meaning in the 1930s, is even found in Dmytryk's *Behind the Rising Sun* [1943], where he condemns Japanese imperialism and the authoritarian civilization which gives rise to it and threatens American values.

The Nazis constituted another danger which was also violently condemned, but only after the beginning of World War II. The films were often the work of German or Austrian immigrants. When France and England were menaced by Nazism they did not give these immigrants the possibility of producing these films while America did.

Although the great crisis of 1929–32 provided food for cinema scenarios of the 1930s, from 1917 to the end of the 1950s there are very few historians and filmmakers who—even if they lean toward "populism" or the New Deal—are deeply critical about the origins of the poor functioning of American society. Nonetheless, this criticism does appear, in an ironic or perverse way, in great comic works of American cinema, from Charlie Chaplin to the Marx Brothers. The same criticism may be glimpsed in a certain way in a number of later comedies, notably those of Preston Sturges. Frank Capra's films, however, recuperate everything and identify themselves totally with the American system which is always legitimized and finally glorified (see *Mr. Smith Goes to Washington* [1939]). It is not surprising that when war broke out Roosevelt made a direct appeal to Capra to bring life to the production of the patriotic films in the "Why We Fight" series and others that he supervised.

This period, which began in 1917, went on for several years after World War II. The victorious Americans had good reasons to attribute their success to their system and their vision of the world. During the McCarthy era films that had formerly glorified America's allies (for example the Soviet Union) were considered suspect. Filmmakers were harassed who were accused of having urged America to go to war less from hatred of Nazism than from solidarity with Communism. This immediate postwar period, which coincides with the beginning of the Cold War, is one where an *official*, obligatory ideology exists. It was the only moment in the history of American cinema where any questioning was identified with treason. Under these conditions, it is understandable that filmmakers had to escape toward "safe" areas: musical comedies, westerns, and gangster films of the sort where "crime doesn't pay"; or else toward films on the Bible, pre-Christian civilizations, and the Roman Empire (the archetype of the American empire). It was not until Stanley Kubrick's *Spartacus* [1960] that revolt and revolution were glorified.

The *fourth stratum* is associated with those who were not satisfied with the ideology of the melting pot and the glorification of American democracy. This ideology corresponds of course to the needs of military leaders and powerful sectors of society, that is, white Anglo-Saxon Protestants. In reality, non-whites, Italians, slaves, Catholics, and Jews found themselves excluded from the American establishment. They were the first to question the ideology of the melting pot and the self-satisfaction of the system in power. Charlie Chaplin shows with bitterness and humor the cruelty of this society, too smug to realize that his image of it is derogatory. In their way, too, Jews—the Marx Brothers and, more recently, Jerry Lewis and Woody Allen—use jokes and humor, the only authorized way of criticizing the establishment.

All the same, the first social group to react as such were blacks, for whom the official discourse about American democracy was nothing but a mockery, a lie. Moreover, they did not take long to observe that in American cinema they played servants or singers, who were often slow-witted. For these reasons, as early as 1920, a black cinema of protest was born which tried to present a "black" vision of American society. *The Birth of a Race* [Emmett Scott] in 1918 was in some sense the first historical *counterfilm* in American cinema. It was followed by many others, such as *Birthright* [Oscar Micheaux, 1924], and *Thousands Cheer* [George Sidney, 1943]. But even among blacks this first wave of black counterfilms was not successful because they were depicted as so honest, just, and virtuous that the films, oozing boredom and morality, did not attract viewers.

Only the second wave of black films—made during the 1970s—was successful, because they combined spectacle, violence, and racial revenge: white women letting themselves go with black males and preferring them to whites; white males finding happiness only with black heroines. Blacks were thus the first to incarnate a new vision of history—opposed to the ideology of the melting pot, this vision could be what Frances Fitzgerald calls the ideology of the salad bowl.

From this point on each ethnic and cultural group glorified its own identity and legitimized its raison d'être. After blacks, or contemporaneously with them, other minorities did the same, notably Jews with Yiddish films. However, the point of view in these films was more ethnographic, not dominated by the spirit of protest.

Above all, after World War II, existing restrictions appeared out of place seeing that new social groups—especially *young people*—forcefully protested against the American family, home, small-town life. The glorification of these had constituted a quasi obligatory leitmotif during the war years and the immediate postwar period, from Sam Wood's *Our Town* [1940], to *Since You Went Away* [John Cromwell, 1944] (with Jennifer Jones), to the very successful *Claudia* [Edmund Goulding, 1943].

Even earlier films had shown some signs of a turn toward a critical vision concerning the war, with the operation of the army and its famous democratic spirit strangely put into question during an era where the army appeared untouchable. Fred Zinnemann's 1953 *From Here to Eternity*, crowned by fifteen prizes, evoked—courageously for its era—the cruelties that can be inflicted in the American army where, needless to say, right (le bon droit) carries the day. But more than the military, it was the family that became the special object of romantic attacks (which cinema glorified) from the world of the young. From *The Wild One* [Laslo Benedek] in 1954 to *Rebel Without a Cause* [Nicholas Ray, 1955] and other films with James Dean, right up to *Bonnie and Clyde* [Arthur Penn, 1967], there have been countless films which express the revolt of youth, the condemnation of the hypocrisy of marriage, and similar themes.

In addition to criticizing the military, the family, or the press (for instance, Billy Wilder's *The Big Carnival* [1951]), a whole series of films has protested about the racism which has victimized Indians and the social segregation endured by women: from Losey's *The Lawless* [1950] to Biberman's *Salt of the Earth* [1955], which combine class struggle, the Indians' struggle for liberty, and the fight for women's liberation. The ideological cast even of Westerns veers around notably at the time of the Vietnam war. The Indian appears as the damaged conscience of citizens, and the American as the imperialist conquerer without faith or law. (All by himself, Elia Kazan is doubtless the filmmaker who has written the most systematic counterhistory of American society from *On the Waterfront* [1954] through *The Visitors* [1972]).

Thus, while schools, novels, and plays (like this protest cinema) present the cultural and historical identity of non-WASPS, the counterhistory of dominant WASP society is analyzed more deeply by film than in novels or textbooks. Following the recession in 1973 (as after the 1929–30 crash), the cinema (this time like the novel) signals—by a movement of return to both catastrophe films and science-fiction films—the appearance of a new vision of History, one that will be drawn by the future.

Thus we have witnessed a reversal or complete rupture of the vision of History, a reversal which peaked at the end of the 1960s and during the 1970s. A very good expression of a movement that characterized all aspects of American life, film gave it an extra corrosiveness. America has been questioning itself more than ever since the Vietnam War. This interrogation is a sign of liberty, a safeguard against a return to the satisfied and chilly conformity of the second third of the twentieth century.

(1984)

CHAPTER 15

The "Fait Divers" and the Writing of History in Fritz Lang's *M*

If a domain exists where cinema has enhanced our understanding of social and political problems, it is those films that tackle a "fait divers" (an accident, crime, disaster, theft, etc.).[1] Cinema has overtaken the novel in this area and, consequently, has enlarged the field of the analysis of societies.

Historians and political scientists usually study problems linked to institutions and political organizations as well as problems of power or counterpower, or else they focus on the study of decisions, of global reactions to the actions and speeches of a regime. Individual cases do not concern them much, unless such cases involve leaders or those who bring about great events. As for sociologists, they are more disposed to study groups, ensembles, systems, or even the functionings of a society. But the minor social fact, which sometimes concerns only one or two people and which does not change the course of history or modify global structures, has been ignored for a long time by the social sciences (with the exception, of course, of certain psychoanalysts). This omission includes "faits divers," these orphans of history.

True, the nineteenth-century novel as well as the turn-of-

154

the-century newspaper serial (like certain television series) were wild about "faits divers." But above all, it is cinema which has been able to make the most of them—and with great success. In fact, the filmed "fait divers" allows the viewer to imagine that he or she participates and plays a role; if one cannot identify with one of the principals one can at least be a Peeping Tom. Moreover, when important people are involved—political figures, high-ranking judges, film stars—they are reduced to the common measure. Thus, the cinematic "fait divers" offers a gourmet feast for those who have only their own history, that is, the dreary repetition of everyday events.

Sometimes cinema is content to reproduce a sensational story—that of Jack the Ripper or Landru—merely creating a work of reconstitution. At other times, when the description of the "fait divers" serves as a sign or symptom of a larger picture or problem, cinema achieves a true work of analysis. Renoir's pre-1939 pioneering works (notably *The Crime of Monsieur Lange* [1935] and *Rules of the Game* [1939]) fall into this latter category, as do Italian neorealist films made between 1945 and 1955 and the French New Wave films of the 1960s, notably those by Chabrol and Godard. Other examples of this category also exist in Japan and in the United States. But the pioneer, the examplary master of this type of film, was Fritz Lang in *M* [1931].

M's story, inspired by a real "fait-divers," is well known: little girls are murdered by a sadist who terrorized the town of Dusseldorf in the late 1920s. The police look everywhere but they are impotent, and the underworld syndicate gets involved because with all the agitation it can no longer "work in peace." With the help of the organization of beggars, the underworld finds the criminal, grabs him, and condemns him to death. But the police, who also know who he is, intervene to prevent the execution and bring the criminal to justice.

Film historians (expecially since Kracauer) have seen this film as the reflection of a society in which the gang members represent the Nazi party and their chief, Schrenke, represents Hitler. Furthermore, both the film and Schrenke exerted a certain fascination on the Führer. A careful look at newsreels between 1931 and 1934 even reveals that Hitler often adopted Schrenke's gestures and attitudes, such as the way he placed his

elbow or broke off his speech abruptly. The filmmaker also fasci-
nated the Führer, for, as we know, Hitler in 1933 proposed that
Fritz Lang—despite his Jewishness—head the German cinema.
Lang refused, preferring to emigrate.

A (Nazi) counter-society in the heart of the Weimar Republic has, as a homologue, the counter-society of the cinematic
gang, which bears no negative connotation in the film. Was not a
criminal, Horst Wessel, the hero of the Nazi hymn? In the film,
the gang is organized in a hierarchical way, and its members are
clear-sighted. The State, on the other hand, inspires neither confidence nor respect. This criminal counter-society could replace
the other for it is certainly its equal. This is the meaning of the
famous parallel montage in which the two groups—the police
and the criminals—try simultaneously and concurrently (but unbeknownst to each other) to find out how to capture the criminal.

The film also raises the problem of individual responsibility
and collective justice. A criminal because he does not control his
impulses, M comes to our attention because he is sick—and, in
their own way, so are the criminals. But the court of criminals,
which embodies popular sentiment, does not see why he should
be judged in these terms. The criminals insist that this sick man,
if locked up and then freed, could begin to kill again. They are in
favor of executing him immediately. Similarly, after 1933, the
Nazi state would exterminate the weak and the handicapped,
insisting that the money spent to cure such people would be spent
in vain and could be put to better use if it were given to healthy
people so that they could buy homes and Volkswagens. Following directions given by Fritz Lang or his companion Thea von
Harbou (who was a Nazi), the film ends on these words after the
police have arrested M, "And now we had better watch over our
children." These words, signaling a distrust of the democratic
institutions of the Weimer Republic, thus clearly attest to the
film's ideology. The plebians in power do not claim to apply the
Rights of Man or the principles of 1789.

Another interesting element appears in Fritz Lang's analysis. If the parallel montage clearly reveals that the two societies—
each with its own code of honor and methods—are at once similar and different, we see also that the systems employed by each
do not function the same way. The State and the police base

themselves on the most scientific and sophisticated methods: first geometry and then chemistry give results that are tested and exploited. The institution thus makes use of technology and knowledge. Quite the contrary is true of the gang members and beggars, who employ their instincts, the occult, and hidden traces. So it happens that it is a blind man whose acute ears recognize a whistled melody, allowing him to discover the guilty person.

This filmic analysis—which reveals the opposition between Instincts and Institution—glorifies a kind of counter-culture of people on the fringes, as well as a return to an instinctive vitality that is natural and free, impeded only by democratic institutions which are impotent and lacking in credibility.

Thus, in *M*, the "fait divers"—which provides the story line—becomes, sometimes through images, sometimes through the sound track, the pretext for an analysis (partly deliberate and partly unconscious) on the part of Fritz Lang. Later on, Lang recounted that when his first wife died and he was found in the arms of Thea von Harbou, he was suspected of being involved in his wife's death. "We could all find ourselves one day in a similar situation," he said; "that's why I'm interested in murder." In retrospect, we can see that if Fritz Lang's life-long obsession with murder (like the problem of denunciation for Kazan) was linked to personal experience, the study of "faits divers" reveals that his artistic vision was that of a scientific observer. For this reason, he was the first of the filmmaker-historians.

(1987)

NOTES

1. [Translator's note: A "fait divers" usually refers to a relatively minor event, treated journalistically as a piece of local news, which often involves something criminal.]

CHAPTER 16

Does a Filmic Writing of History Exist?

The problem is whether or not cinema and television modify our vision of History, given that History concerns not only knowledge of past phenomena, but also the analysis of links between past and present, the search for continuities and ruptures.

There is no doubt that in the last decades this problem has assumed a new importance. The time spent watching television keeps growing in Western societies where television has become a kind of "parallel school." Moreover, for people who were colonized (especially those who do not have a written historical tradition), historical knowledge depends even more than elsewhere on the media, even if they have a strong oral tradition. Clearly, the stakes posed here are high.

Nonetheless, the problem is not entirely new. As information or knowledge, historical science has already been confronted with problems of the same nature. Novels and plays have triumphed over historical knowledge, at least in our diffuse memories. When we think of Cardinal Richelieu or Cardinal Mazarin, are not the first memories that come to mind drawn from Alexandre Dumas's *The Three Musketeers?* The same holds true of England where, as Peter Saccio has shown, everything Shakespeare says about Joan of Arc is invented and yet, despite the work of historians, it is Shakespeare's Joan of Arc that the English remember. The more time that passes, the less historians can change that.

Unlike a work of history, which necessarily changes with distance and analytical developments, a work of art becomes permanent, unchanging. If these works of art are numerous the problem remains. The case of Napoleon in Russia is a good example. In that country, where the figure of Napoleon has exerted a greater fascination than elsewhere, what image of him wins out among so many different portraits? Is he an antichrist, a barbarian, a tyrant, a Prometheus, a martyr, a genius, or a mysterious phantom? Is he Pushkin's epic hero, Dostoevsky's or Tolstoy's philosophical given, the Marxists' proof? Which of these wins out? Certainly not the figure drawn by historians.

Today cinema and television constitute a new form of expression for history. How does this form contribute to and transform our understanding of history?

The case of *Battleship Potemkin* is linked to this problem. Are not the images of the Revolution of 1905 which dominate our memory those from Eisenstein's work? Like the snowball scene in Gance's *Napoléon*, most of the scenes in these films stem only from the director's imagination. The ideological impact of these masterpieces, the stakes represented by these films, have been such that we have long been afraid to analyze them. That would have been sacrilegious toward those who consider the cinema a new Revelation.

In fact there are several ways to look at a historical film. The most common of these, inherited from the tradition of scholarship, consists in verifying if the reconstruction is precise (are the soldiers of 1914 mistakenly wearing helmets which were introduced only after 1916?), seeing that the décor and the location is faithful and the dialogue is authentic. For the most part filmmakers pay attention to this scholarly precision. In order to guarantee it they happily turn to counterfeit historians who get lost deep down in the list of credits. Obviously there are more demanding filmmakers who go to the archives themselves and play at being historians. They try to supply an ancient feel to the dialogue, by using the patois of Silesia (Peter Fleischmann), the language of the Camisards [René Allio]. The fame of some directors (like Bertrand Tavernier) comes from this demanding approach. Still others, such as Bernardo Bertolucci in *La Strategia del Ragno* [*The Spider's Strategem*, 1970], know how to use a simple red scarf or an indefinable change in luminosity to represent the passage to a far-off past or to an imaginary world.

The scholarly, positivist approach does not exclude the use of other criteria. The realization of *Alexander Nevsky* and *Andrei Rubylov*, for example, is due to two artists [Eisenstein and Tarkovsky] who both make these scholarly demands. Nonetheless, they recreate the same (or almost the same) moments of history by making two films with opposite meanings. In *Nevsky* the mortal enemy is the Germans, the Teutons; in *Rubylov* it is the Chinese, the Tartars. In *Rubylov* Russia is saved by her sanctity, her Christianity; in *Nevsky* the hero is deliberately secularized. Taking this for granted we quickly separate the film's ideology from the filmmaker's talent.

The ideological view often supplants the positivist one; the film is appreciated for its meaning as well as for its essence. In a society dominated by ideology it is easy to see why this way of seeing gained the upper hand. It is obvious that Abel Gance and Jean Renoir offer two contrary visions of the French Revolution. Gance's is Bonapartist and pre-Fascist, glorifying the man of destiny; Renoir's is Marxian and ignores even the existence of great men. In each case, and without having to justify or legitimize his choice, the filmmaker chooses those historical facts and elements that provide fodder for his demonstration, leaving out the others. This makes him happy as well as those who share his faith and who constitute "his public." If the cause he defends is widely shared, it is to the benefit of both the filmmaker's prestige and his financial rewards. But it may not necessarily benefit historical analysis—the intelligibility of the phenomena.

From this point of view Stanley Kubrick's *Paths of Glory* constitutes quite a problematic case. Unravelling the motives for an offensive-at-any-price (with all the rottenness that this involves from the top to the bottom of the military hierarchy), its choice of situations—all authentic—is such that it pleases anti-militarists, democrats, and those on the Left. Nonetheless, it heaps up so many abuses that it neutralizes the credibility of the overall view and renders incomprehensible the birth and durability of veteran's groups where—for a long time after 1918—soldiers and officers continued to fraternize.

All this reveals that the historical film (or, more often, the film about history) is no more than the filmic transcription of a vision of history which has been conceived by others.

Doubtless through an innovative choice of a particular story, some filmmakers help render intelligible certain historical phenomena and they do so in a creative fashion. For example, in *La Caduta degli Dei* [*The Damned*, 1969], Luchino Visconti opens a royal way for those who want to understand how Nazism penetrated into the German upper bourgeoisie. Moreover, in this case the form and theme chosen cloud the film's latent ideology—an ideology which is that of Visconti himself, who sees the meaning of history as a kind of decadence. As Ishaghpour has shown in his 1984 publication, each of Visconti's works constitutes an elegy for everything that disappears forever under the force of the new.

The case is different for all these films which use incidental events ("fait divers") to indicate social and political functioning. In this, Renoir, Rossellini, Godard, and Chabrol have followed in the path of novelists such as Zola or Sartre, only these filmmakers have applied this procedure to the past (not only to the present), and they have outpaced historians.

Thus, since any theme can be manipulated, the principal distinction is not really between films where history provides the setting (such as *La grande illusion* or *Gone With the Wind*) and those whose subject is history (such as *Danton*). The distinction is rather between films inscribed in the flow of dominant (or oppositional) currents of thought and those that propose an independent or innovative view of societies.

Thus the function of analysis, or counteranalysis, in cinema can only really take place on two conditions. First, filmmakers must have separated themselves from ideological forces and ruling institutions (and this is not the case of directors of propaganda films). If not, their work only furthers, in a new form, dominant (or oppositional) ideological currents. A second condition is obviously that the writing be cinematic (and not, for example, filmed theater) and that it use specific cinematic means. The contribution of cinema to the intelligibility of historical phenomena varies according to the degree of its autonomy and its esthetic contribution.

Whether dealing with the history of great men (Nevsky, Napoleon, General Custer) or favoring the action of groups (Pudovkin's *Mother*, Renoir's *La Marseillaise*), these films reproduce dominant (or oppositional) currents of thought. The pleasure they evoke through their beauty is the only way that can act upon society, upon history—even if it is not what was desired. For example, in making *La grande illusion* Renoir wanted to act *upon* history, to act for peace. Films in this category go a bit further when the artist does not merely reconstitute a phenomenon but "reconstructs" it. This is the case in *Strike*, where Eisenstein achieves a filmic transcription of a Marxist analysis of a pre-1905 Russian factory.

Films which still involve collective struggle, but which are designed to fight the dominant system, are set under the contrary sign since they go against the current or reigning power. The contribution of films such as Herbert J. Biberman's *Salt of the Earth* [1953], the majority of Polish historical films, and *Andrei Rubylov* or *Ceddo* [Sembène Ousmane, 1978] is superb. These films not only bear witness but are involved in the struggle.

It seems appropriate to place to one side those films that stem both from an analysis independent of any [ideological] affiliation and at the same time use specifically filmic means of expression. A typical example of this category seems to be Fritz Lang's *M* [1931]. Through the story of a psychotic it shows how the Weimar Republic functioned. The use of parallel montage, the alternation of sound and image give the narration a form which can be found only in cinema. Its idea, like its analytical procedures, is both innovating and independent.

M constitutes one example. But there are many other films which contribute to an understanding of societies. One could mention the work of Elia Kazan, of Renoir, or of the New Wave, which—thanks to incidental events—has been able to go ahead with a social analysis of the present time, a time also rooted in the heritage of the past.

In addition to documentary films, which preserve the image

of the present, as well as what remains of the past, or which use the memory of societies (such as Jean Rouch's *Babatu* [1976]) one can also place to one side those filmmakers who offer a global interpretation of history—an interpretation which springs solely from their own analysis and which is no longer merely a reconstruction or a reconstitution, but really an original contribution to the understanding of past phenomena and their relation to the present. However one feels about the validity of their analyses, the works of Hans Jurgen Syberberg, Tarkovsky, and Visconti come into this category.

Proposition for a Global Classification of Films in Their Relationship to History, Followed by a Model

It appears, then, that statements about society come from four impulses:

1) Dominant institutions and ideologies, which may express the point of view of the state, a church, a party, or any organization having its own vision of the world.

2) Those opposed to this vision, who elaborate a counterhistory or a counteranalysis, insofar as they have the means and the ability to do so.

3) Social or historical memory, which survives through oral tradition or through legitimized works of art.

4) Independent interpretations—scientific or not—which proceed with their own analysis.

A second mode of classifying films and other cultural works concerns their mode of approach. Do they approach social and historical problems:

1) From above—that is, from the viewpoint of power and its demands?

2) From below—are questions analyzed from the viewpoint of the masses—peasants, workers, fishermen?

3) The third mode attacks the phenomena from within. The narrator places himself into his analysis keeping pace with the object of his study. This occurs when the filmmaker clarifies his procedure through a voice-over or chats with his camera (Dziga Vertov in *Man with a Camera*).

Centers of Production / Modes of Analysis	INSTITUTIONS OFFICIAL HISTORY	COUNTER INSTITUTIONS	MEMORIES	AUTONOMOUS ANALYSES
FROM ABOVE	*Napoléon** *Alexander Nevsky*	*Ceddo* *The Black Hills Are Not For Sale*	no	Visconti Syberberg
FROM BELOW	*La Marseillaise* *Mother* (Pudovkin)	Feminist films Ivens 1938	*Babatu*	*The Bicycle Thief* *Modern Times* *A nous la liberté*
FROM WITHIN	*Man with a Camera*	*The Salt of the Earth*	*Femmes du mont Chenoua**	no
FROM WITHOUT	*Strike* *Gestern und Heute* (Nazi)	Polish historical films	no	*M** *The Visitors* New Wave (France) Renoir

*Cinematographic writing plays a special role.

4) The fourth mode of approach tackles problems by constructing models from without, by formally reconstructing a social or political object without trying to reconstitute it.

These four modes and approaches allow us to propose a general model of classification. Nonetheless, it must first be remarked that a work, filmic or not, can involve several of these modes and approaches. It is up to the analysis to identify its characteristics; this proposal for classification only plays an instrumental role. For example, Biberman's *Salt of the Earth* is a film which both questions the official vision of history, and approaches society from below, analyzing the behavior of Indian miners and their wives. It is a work that calls upon witnesses and their memories. But it is also a work that reconstructs the exemplary model of a strike where the workers struggle against a big company. The Indians are against their Yankee patrons, while the men fight against a movement instigated by their wives.

(1978)

FILMS CITED

A *nous la liberté*, René Clair (France, 1931). Explores the benefits of automation through the story of a prison escapee who becomes an industrial magnate. Will the machine liberate man?

Alexander Nevsky, Sergei Eisenstein (U.S.S.R., 1938). Russia's struggle against the Teutonic Knights.

Andrei Rubylov, Andrei Tarkovsky (U.S.S.R., 1966). The artist's struggle for freedom of expression.

Babatu, Jean Rouch (France, 1976). An African village reconstructs the end of its struggle against European invaders at the start of the twentieth century.

The Black Hills Are Not For Sale, S. Osawa (U.S.A., 1978). How General Custer violated the treaty of Laramie in 1868; a questioning of official history.

Ceddo, Sembène Ousmane (Senegal, 1978). The struggle of an African village against Islamization at the end of the nineteenth century.

Dura Lex [*Po zakonu (By the Law)*], Lev Kuleshov (U.S.S.R., 1926). Soviet justice is called into question by means of a western set in Canada.

Femmes du mont Chenoua, Assia Djebar (Algeria, 1980). A woman fighter tells how she believed that the struggle for independence would mean female emancipation.

Gestern und Heute [*Yesterday and Today*], (Nuremberg, 1934). A parallel study of the sufferings of Germany during the Weimar Republic and its achievements under Nazism.

Heimat, Edgar Reitz (West Germany, 1984). The Weimar era and the Nazi era seen through the experiences of a German family.

Hitler, Hans Jurgen Syberberg (West Germany, 1978). A philosopher and psychiatrist analyzes the case of Hitler in the framework of German history.

Ivan's Childhood [*Ivanovo detstvo*], Andrei Tarkovsky (U.S.S.R., 1962). A child's view of World War II.

La grande illusion [*Grand Illusion*], Jean Renoir (France, 1938). A prisoner of war camp during World War I.

La Marseillaise [*The Marseillaise*], Jean Renoir (France, 1938). A Marxist interpretation of the French Revolution.

Ladri di Biciclette [*The Bicycle Thief*], Vittorio de Sica (Italy, 1948). The drama of a man who is out of work, caught stealing, and is arrested in front of his little boy.

M, Fritz Lang (Germany, 1932). An analysis of German society through a minor incident.

Man with a Camera [*Chelovek S Kinoapparatom*], Dziga Vertov (U.S.S.R., 1929). A montage of shots of contemporary Russia; a formal experiment.

Modern Times, Charlie Chaplin (U.S.A., 1936). The Little Tramp versus the System.

Mother [*Mat*], Vsevold Pudovkin (U.S.S.R., 1926). The birth of revolutionary consciousness.

Napoléon, Abel Gance (France, 1926). The rise of a hero facing the revolution.

Salt of the Earth, Herbert J. Biberman (U.S.A., 1953). A strike of Indian women in the West.

Strike [*Satchka*], Sergei Eisenstein (U.S.S.R., 1925). The "model" of a strike under Czarism.

The Visitors, Elia Kazan (U.S.A., 1972). Should one denounce a friend who is guilty of a war crime?

BIBLIOGRAPHY

This bibliography is devoted to works specifically within the framework of "cinema and history." It therefore excludes classical works on the history of cinema (by Kracauer, Bardèche, Sadoul, etc.) as well as dictionaries, reviews, and reference works (*Cahiers du cinéma, Positif, Variety, Ciné-action*), or monographs or autobiographies on the part of filmmakers or participants (Lotte Eisner's *Fritz Lang*, Raoul Walsh's *Hollywood*). It focuses on works which appeared after the French edition of Marc Ferro's *Cinéma et histoire*, published by DeNoel Gonthier in 1977.

The numbers 1–4 in parentheses indicate which axis or part of this study the work in question most closely involves:
1) Film: source of history;
2) Film: agent of history;
3) Modes of action of cinematographic language;
4) Society which produces, society which receives.

Journals
Historical Journal of Film, Radio, and Television. Oxford, U.K.: Carfax Publishing Company.
Film and History. Newark: New Jersey Institute of Technology.
Newsletter. Copenhagen: International Association for Audiovisual Media in Historical Research and Education.
Film et Histoire. Paris: Ecole des Hautes Études en Sciences Sociales.
Cahiers de la Cinémathèque. Perpignan: Palais des Congrès.

Books and Articles
Aldgate, Anthony. *Cinema and History: British Newsreels and the Spanish Civil War.* London: Scholar Press, 1979. (1,2)
Barco del Rio, Ramon. *Historia a traves del cine.* Madrid: Artedita, 1976. (1)
Ceplair, Larry, and Steven Englund. *The Inquisition in Hollywood: Politics in the Film Community, 1930–1960.* Berkeley, Ca.: University of California Press, 1983. (2)
Ferro, Marc. *Analyse de film, analyse de société.* Paris: Hachette, 1976. (1)
Fledelius, Karsten, and K. R. M. Short, eds. *History and Film Methodology, Research, Education.* Proceedings of the 8th International Conference

166

on History and the Audio-Visual Media, Amersfoot, September, 1979. Copenhagen: Eventus, 1980. (1, 3)

France, Claudine de. *Cinéma et anthropologie*. Paris: Maison des Sciences de l'Homme, 1984. (3)

Friedman, R. M. *L'Image et son Juif: le Juif dans le cinéma nazi*. Paris: Payot, 1983. (1, 2)

Garçon, François. *De Blum à Petain: cinéma et société française (1936–1940)*. Preface by Marc Ferro. Paris: Editions du Cerf, 1984. (1)

Gheorghiu-Cernat, Manuela. *Arms and Films*. Bucharest: Meridiane, 1983. (1, 2)

Gili, Jean. *Stato fascista e cinematografia: repressione e promozione*. Rome: Bulzoni, 1981. (2)

Goldmann, Annie. *Cinéma et société moderne: le Cinéma de 1958 à 1968*. Paris: Denoel, 1967. (1, 4)

———. *L'Errance dans le cinéma contemporain*. Paris: Verrier, 1985. (1,4)

Hockings, P., ed. *Principles of Visual Anthropology*. The Hague: Mouton, 1975. (3)

Kenez, Peter. *The Birth of the Propaganda State: Soviet Methods of Mass Mobilization, 1917–1929*. Cambridge: Cambridge University Press, 1985. (2)

Lera, Jose M. Caparros. *Arte y Politica en el Cine de la Republica (1931–1939)*. Barcelona: Edic. Universidad, 1981. (1)

O'Connor, John, and M. Jackson. *American History, American Film: Interpreting the Hollywood Image*. New York: Ungar, 1979. (1)

Pithon, Remy. "Le film comme document historique et sociologique." *Revue européenne des Sciences Morales et Cahiers Pareto* 13 (1973). (1)

Pronay, N., and D. W. Spring, eds. *Propaganda, Politics, and Film, 1918–1945*. London: Macmillan, 1982. (1, 2)

Richards, Jeffrey. *Visions of Yesterday*. London: Routledge & Kegan Paul, 1973. (1)

———. *The Age of the Dream Palace: Cinema and Society in Britain, 1930–1939*. London: Routledge & Kegan Paul, 1984. (1)

Rimberg, J. D. *The Motion Picture in the Soviet Union, 1918–1952: A Sociological Analysis*. New York: Arno Press, 1973. (1–4)

Short, K. R. M., ed. *Feature Films as History*. Knoxville: University of Tennessee Press, 1981. (1)

Smith, Paul, ed. *The Historian and Film*. Cambridge: Cambridge University Press, 1976. (1)

Sorlin, Pierre. *Sociologie du cinéma*. Paris: Aubier, 1977. (1–4)

———. *The Film in History: Restaging the Past*. Totowa, N.J.: Barnes & Noble, 1980. (1–4)

Taylor, Robert. *Film Propaganda, Soviet Russia and Nazi Germany*. London: Croom Helm, 1979. (1, 2)

Thorpe, F., and N. Pornay, with Clive Coultass. *British Official Films in the Second World War: A Descriptive Catalogue*. Santa Barbara: Clio Press, 1980. (1,2)

INDEX

Marc Ferro is a professor of history at l'Ecole des Hautes Etudes en Sciences Sociales in Paris, and a Co-Directeur (Editor) of Annales (E.S.C.). His published works include The Great War, 1914–1918; The Russian Revolution of February 1912; The Bolshevik Revolution: A Social History of the Russian Revolution and The Use and Abuse of History, which have appeared in English. His most recent book is Pétain.

Naomi Greene is a professor of French and the chair of the Film Studies Program at the University of California, Santa Barbara. She received her Ph.D. degree from New York University. She is the author of Antonin Artaud: Poet without Words and René Clair: A Guide to References and Resources, and is the translator of Foghorn, a book of poems by Jacques Temple.

The manuscript was prepared for publication by Laurel Brandt and Anne Adamus. The book was designed by Don Ross. The typeface for the text is Electra. The display faces are Broadway and Electra. The book is printed on 60-lb. Arbor text paper and is bound in Holliston Mills' Roxite Vellum.

Manufactured in the United States of America.